MEMORY CULTURE

MEMORY CULTURE

THE SCIENCE OF
Observing, Remembering and Recalling

BY

WILLIAM WALKER ATKINSON

GYAN

Published by

Gyan Publishing House
5, Ansari Road
Daryaganj, New Delhi-110002
Phone: 011-47034999, 9811692060
E-mail: books@gyanbooks.com

Distribution Network
gyanbooks.com
India, USA, Canada, UK, Australia

ISBN: 978-93-6208-371-5 (PB)
First Published, 1903

2nd Impression 2024

Printed at: Gyan Press, Delhi.

MEMORY CULTURE
Author: WILLIAM WALKER ATKINSON

MEMORY CULTURE

THE SCIENCE OF

Observing, Remembering and Recalling

By

WILLIAM WALKER ATKINSON

OF THE PENNSYLVANIA BAR;

Author of THOUGHT FORCE; LAW OF THE NEW THOUGHT, Etc.

"As wax to receive—as adamant to retain."

Published by

THE PSYCHIC RESEARCH COMPANY

3835 Vincennes Avenue

CHICAGO

1903

Contents.

CHAPTER I.

The Subconscious Storehouse 7

Treating of the great subconscious region of the mind lying outside the field of consciousness, which region is the home of the memory, the storehouse of impressions received through the senses. The relation of the memory to this great storehouse is discussed, and numerous examples and illustrations are given, showing that nothing is ever forgotten, and how apparently forgotten facts may be recalled under certain circumstances. Our impressions lie hidden in the deep recesses of the subconscious mentality awaiting the hour of their voluntary or involuntary revival. The study of this chapter will throw new light on the subject of Memory Culture.

CHAPTER II.

Attention and Concentration 12

Treating of the law of pyschology that the intensity of the original impression determines the degree of future remembrance or recollection, and that the intensity of the original impression is proportionate to the attention given the subject or object producing the impression. Showing how the subconscious mentality stores away the impressions received, and how those which are carefully stored away may be more easily found and brought into the field of consciousness. Examples and illustrations are given, and the matter of attention, interest and concentration is discussed in their relation to Memory Culture.

CHAPTER III.

Acquiring Impressions 17

Treating of the laws governing the acquiring of impressions—how impressions may be clearly received and retained—the difference between voluntary attention and involuntary attention—how sense impressions are received—how the senses may be trained to readily receive and store away impressions—the necessity of careful observation, etc., etc., etc. Numerous illustrations are given showing the wonderful degree of perception, observation and memory attained by persons in all ages and countries, by careful and intelligent practice. Remarkable instances and interesting anecdotes are given, to illustrate the subject discussed in this chapter.

CHAPTER IV.

Eye Perception and Memory 25

Treating of the receiving of impressions through the sense of sight—the vital importance of the training of the eye to receive impressions clearly and distinctly—the benefit of such training in every day and business life—the importance of such training in Memory Culture. Showing that the majority of people "look at" rather than "see" things. Interesting examples and illustrations are given, showing how this faculty has been developed by those who have devoted attention to the subject, and the general rules governing the development and cultivation of this faculty of the mind are given.

CHAPTER V.

Exercises in Eye Perception 31

Treating of the means whereby the faculty of careful observation and clear-seeing may be developed and cultivated, to the end that the student may be able to receive and store away clear and distinct impressions of the things coming before his sight. Interesting and useful exercises are given to aid the student in "the art of seeing," which exercises, if carefully practiced, will develop the faculty of observation to a wonderful extent, and will not only greatly improve the memory, but will make the student a careful observer and improve his general usefulness. The importance of the subject is not generally understood.

CHAPTER VI.

EAR PERCEPTION AND MEMORY 36

Treating of the receiving of impressions through the sense of hearing—the advantages of cultivating this faculty—the rules governing same—instances of wonderful ear perception and memory, etc., etc., etc. This phase of the subject is one which usually receives but scant attention from students, and yet some of the most remarkable instances of memory development depended upon the cultivation and development of "ear attention." For long ages, the religious, philosophical, and legal teachings of ancient races were transmitted from mouth to ear, the memory performing feats now deemed almost incredible, but which may be reproduced by any one devoting sufficient attention to the subject.

CHAPTER VII.

EXERCISES IN EAR PERCEPTION 40

Treating of the development of ear perception and memory, following the preceding chapter, and giving numerous exercises designed to develop and cultivate the faculty of intelligent hearing. Instances of greatly developed ear perception show us that the majority of people have the sense of hearing but imperfectly developed, and place but little attention upon what they hear, and that this faculty may be greatly developed and improved by intelligent practice. Good authorities have stated that "one-half of the deafness that exists is the result of inattention," and one-half of the poor memories are traceable to the same cause. The exercises are designed to remedy this defect. This chapter includes a valuable system for memorizing things heard, following the lines laid down by the ancient Hindu teachers when transmitting their sacred teachings.

CHAPTER VIII.

ASSOCIATION 46

Treating of that great law of the mind, upon which depends very much of the faculty of recalling, known as Association. The sequence of our thoughts is as much the result of a law as is the rising and falling of the tides. Our thoughts and recorded impressions are always associated in some way, although sometimes it is difficult to trace the connection. This chapter discusses the subject of Association, showing the several forms and the rules governing each. Next to Attention, this subject is the most important feature of Memory Culture, and the subject itself is full of interest and opens up a great field of thought.

CHAPTER IX.

REMEMBRANCE, RECOLLECTION AND RECOGNITION 50

Treating of these three operations of the mind, which are frequently considered as being the same thing. The differences are pointed out, and each term is clearly defined and explained. Remembrance is the word meaning that process of the memory whereby stored impressions come again into the field of consciousness without an effort of the will, as by association, resemblance, etc. Recollection is the word used to describe that process of the memory whereby a thing is recalled by an effort of the will. Recognition is that process of memory whereby, when we see or hear a thing, we know that we have seen or heard it before.

CHAPTER X.

General Principles Regarding Impressions........................ 54

Treating of the thirteen general principles governing the subject of impressions. These thirteen principles practically sum up the entire subject of impressions, their acquirement, their retention, their recalling; and the knowledge of the same will enable the student to have the entire subject in a nutshell. Each principle is clearly stated, and is accompanied with explanations and illustrations. This chapter alone, if carefully studied, will give the student a liberal education in the theory and practice of Memory Culture, and might readily be expanded to fill a book.

CHAPTER XI.

The Cumulative System of Memory Culture........................ 61

Treating of a rational, practical, easily acquired system of Memory Culture, which in the opinion of the author of this book is the best and only practical method of developing the Memory as a whole. This is a modern presentation of the system used by the ancients, in India, Greece, Iceland, and other countries, to train the minds of students that they might acquire and store away the legends, religious books, philosophies, and laws of the races, and by means of which it was a common thing for these pupils to memorize books exceeding in size our Bible. Full instructions and directions are given for the development of the memory by this great system.

CHAPTER XII.

The Ten-Question Thought System............................ 67

Treating of a novel and rational method of bringing forth from the subconscious storehouse the miscellaneous assortment of information which every person has stored away regarding various subjects, but which knowledge is unavailable and unused because of the lack of system in the storing way, and the absence of knowledge of a method whereby this scattered knowledge may be brought together. This system, if mastered and practiced, will immensely increase the available information at the disposal of one, and will render one "well informed" upon subjects of which he apparently knows but little. It is an eye opener, and will produce remarkable results. This chapter also contains an explanation of "Analytical Memorizing."

CHAPTER XIII.

Memory of Figures, Dates and Prices............................ 71

Treating of the development of the memory upon these most interesting lines, which are so important to the man and woman in their everyday and business life. There is nothing so annoying to the student as to forget dates, and the failure to remember prices and figures has proved the undoing of many a promising young business man. This chapter goes into the subject clearly, and gives explanations of poor memory along these lines, and points out the methods whereby improvement may be had. Exercises and directions are given, which will prove valuable to the student.

CHAPTER XIV.

MEMORY OF PLACE.. 75

Treating of that faculty of the mind which when largely developed enables one to find his way almost instinctively in strange places, and which, when deficient, causes one to "get lost" in places with which he should be familiar. The subject is taken up with the idea of showing how the faculty may be developed, and the importance of training and cultivating it. Instruction, examples, and exercises are given upon well tested and tried lines, and the careful study of this chapter should start one well on the road to a great improvement in his sense of location, his memory of places, and the ability to "keep his bearings."

CHAPTER XV.

MEMORY OF FACES.. 78

Treating of the faculty of remembering the faces of those with whom we come in contact. Showing the importance of having a good memory of faces and the embarrassment attendant upon a poor memory of this kind. This chapter takes upon the matter from the cause to the remedy, and a careful study and application of the principles laid down will undoubtedly result in a great improvement along these lines. There is no attempt made to teach any "trick method," the idea followed being that an intelligent training of the faculty must result in an improvement in the faculty itself, which will in turn be the cause of an improved memory of this kind. Exercises are included.

CHAPTER XVI.

MEMORY OF NAMES.. 81

Treating of that most important phase of Memory Culture—the cultivation of the Memory of Faces. This faculty is a most important one to every one in business and public life, and a poor memory for faces has resulted in many cases of active ill-will on the part of those whom one has failed to recognize. This faculty may be trained and developed, as well as others, and this chapter takes up the subject of this development, giving the cause of poor memories of this sort, and the best methods of improving same by training and developing the faculty itself. Examples and exercises are given, which will prove interesting as well as instructive.

CHAPTER XVII.

ARTIFICIAL SYSTEMS 86

Treating of the many artificial systems of memory training which have been offered the public in all ages and among all people, showing the general nature of the principal systems, and calling attention to their weak points. The history of these systems takes the reader back to the time of Simonides, 500 B. C., and shows how the old systems are dressed up and offered as new systems by their "discoverers." This chapter will prove interesting to those who like to go back to the root of things, and then follow up the development of the subject. The reading of this chapter will enable the reader to understand the claims of many of the widely advertised systems and will show him that there is "nothing new under the sun" so far as "patent" systems of memorizing are concerned.

CHAPTER I.

THE SUBCONSCIOUS STOREHOUSE.

Treating of the great subconscious region of the mind, lying outside the field of consciousness, which region is the home of the memory, the storehouse of impression received through the senses—The relation of the memory to this great storehouse is discussed, and numerous examples and illustrations are given, showing that nothing is ever forgotten, and how apparently forgotten facts may be recalled under certain circumstances—Our impressions lie hidden in the deep recesses of the subconscious mentality awaiting the hour of their voluntary or involuntary revival—The study of this chapter will throw new light on the subject of Memory Culture.

We can form no clear conception of the nature of memory, or of the rules governing the faculties of remembrance and recollection, unless we understand something about that great region of the mind known to psychologists as the subconscious field of mentation. It was formerly taught that the mind was conscious of all that went on within itself, but the advanced thought of the age now recognizes that consciousness forms but a small part of the total of mental processes. Subconscious ideas, impressions, sensations and thoughts play a most important part in the world of thought. It is now understood that in every conscious act there is much that belongs to the region of the subconscious. In every conscious act there is a background of subconsciousness.

Back of the field of consciousness lies the great region of subconsciousness. This subconscious region contains many mysteries which are engaging the attention of psychologists and other thinkers, the results of whose investigation and labors are exercising an important influence on the thought of the age. It has been estimated that less than ten per cent of the mental operations of every day life are performed on the conscious plane, the balance of the work being done in the great subconscious regions of the mind. That which we call conscious mentation is but the peaks of submerged mountains, the vast body of the mountains being hidden by the waters. We are as if in a forest in the darkest night, our lantern casting around us a little luminous circle, beyond which is a large ring of twilight, and still beyond this is absolute darkness. And in this twilight, and in this darkness, work is being done, the results of which, when necessary, are pushed forward into the circle of light which we know as consciousness.

Memory is primarily a function of our subconscious mentality. In the great subconscious region lies the great store-house of Memory. From the moment we receive an impression, until the moment when it is again brought into the field of consciousness, the subconscious faculties are at work. We receive and store away an impression—where do we store it? Not in the conscious region, else it were always before us—down in the depths of the subconscious store-house is it stored, placed among other impressions, often so carelessly that we find it almost impossible to find it when again we need it. Where is it kept during the years that often intervene between the storing away of an impression and its subsequent revival? In this great store-house of the subconscious. What process is employed when we wish to recall an impression? Simply an order going forth from the Will, bidding the workers in the subconscious warehouse to find and bring into the light the impression laid away so long ago. And in the degree that these workers have been trained to do their work and accustom themselves to their task, do they succeed in intelligently obeying the orders of the Will. And in the measure that they have been taught to carefully store away the things committed to their charge, and to carefully note the locations of the treasures committed to them, are they apt and quick in bringing them to light when they are bidden.

Consciousness cannot be regarded as synonymous with mind. If we treat consciousness and mind as coextensive, and discard the idea of the subconscious field of mentation, we will be at a loss to explain where, during a particular conscious state, all the rest of the mind is; where are all the other bits of mental furniture other than the particular piece then in use. The field of consciousness at any particular moment is very limited, and reminds one of looking through a telescope or microscope where he sees only that which is within the field of the instrument, all outside of that field being as if it did not exist, for the moment. The mind is constantly filled with ideas, thoughts, impressions, etc., of which we are totally unconscious until they are brought into the field of consciousness.

It is believed that every impression received—every thought that we evolve—every act that we perform—is recorded somewhere in this great subconscious storehouse of the mind, and that nothing is ever absolutely forgotten. Many things that have been apparently forgotten for years, will come into the field of consciousness when summoned there by some association, desire, need or stress. Many mental impressions probably never will be brought again into the field of consciousness, there being no need for such bringing forth, but will remain in the subconscious region silently but powerfully molding our thoughts, ideas and actions. Other impressions will lie hidden in the deep recesses of the mind, awaiting the hour of their renewed use, just as future light and heat lie hidden in the coal in the uncovered strata of the earth's surface, awaiting the time when it will be brought forth for use.

We are at any one time conscious of but a very small part of what is stored away in the mind. Many things which seem to have been forgotten, and which we have often endeavored to recall, will at some time come apparently unbidden into the field of consciousness, as if of its own accord. We often try to recall a thing, but it proves elusive, and we cease our efforts, but after a time, suddenly, the idea flashes forth right in the glare of consciousness. It would seem that our desire for recollection often starts into operation the silent workers of the subconsciousness, and long after, when we have almost forgotten the desire, they return triumphantly dragging the desired impression with them. Then again, a chance word of another may open up vast fields of memory, of whose existence we may have long since lost sight. Often in a dream we will see long forgotten faces, hear and recognize voices whose tones had faded away many years ago. Many events which have been so completely forgotten that no effort of the will seems able to recall them, still seem to be firmy imbedded somewhere in the subconsciousness, and some extraordinary stimulus, strain, or physical condition brings them forth as fresh and vivid as the impression of yesterday.

Persons in the delirium attending fever will often speak of things which they had entirely forgotten, and of which they failed to recall a single particular after their recovery, but which, upon investigation, proved to have actually occurred in their childhood or youth. It is stated that a drowning man will often recall the events of his past life, and many interesting experiences along this line are related in the standard works on the subject of psychology. Sir Francis Beaufort after being rescued from drowning, stated that "every incident of my former life seemed to pass before my recollection in a retrograde succession, not in mere outline, but the picture being filled up with every minute and collateral feature, constituting a kind of panoramic view of my entire existence."

Coleridge relates the tale of a young woman who could neither read nor write, who, being seized with a fever, began talking in Latin, Greek and Hebrew. Whole sheets of her ravings were written out, and were found to consist of sentences intelligible in themselves, but having slight connection with each other. Of her Hebrew sayings only a few could be traced to the Bible, and most seemed to be of Rabbinical dialect. The woman was grossly ignorant, and all trickery seemed out of the question, and she was generally believed to be possessed of a devil. A physician who doubted the theory of demoniacal possession, determined to solve the mystery, and after much trouble discovered that at the age of nine she had been cared for in the household of an old clergyman. The clergyman was in the habit of walking up and down a passage of the house into which the kitchen opened, reciting to himself passages of the Rabbinical writings, and quotations from the Latin and Greek Fathers. His books were examined and every passage which the girl had uttered was found to be therein contained. The fever had caused the subconsciousness storehouse to bring forth some of its oldest treasures.

Carpenter relates the story of an English clergyman who visited a castle of which he had no recollection of having ever seen before. But as he approached the gateway he became conscious of a very vivid impression of having been there before, and seemed to not only see the gateway itself, but donkeys beneath the arch, and people on top of it. He was much wrought up over the matter, and some time afterward inquired of his mother whether she could throw any light upon the subject. She informed him that when he was a little child of but eighteen months of age, she had gone with a large party to that particular castle, and had taken him in the pannier of a donkey; that some of the people took their lunch on the roof of the gateway, while the child had been left below with the attendants and donkeys. On the occasion of the second visit the sight of the gateway brought up all the old childish recollection, although it seemed like a dream.

Abercrombie relates the story of a lady dying in a house in the country. Her infant daughter was brought from London to visit her, and after a short interview returned to town. The mother died, and the infant grew into womanhood without the slightest recollection of her mother. When she was a middle-aged woman she chanced to visit the house in which her mother died, and entered the room itself, although not knowing it to be the one in which the mother had passed away. She started upon entering the room, and when a friend inquired the cause of her agitation, said that she had a most vivid recollection of having been in that room before, and of the fact that a lady who lay in that corner, and who seemed to be very ill, had leaned over her and wept. And so the impression stored away in the subconscious storehouse of that baby brain, had remained there unknown, until its owner had grown to middle-age, when at the sight of the room the impression was revived and memory gave up some of its secrets.

There are the best possible grounds for asserting that nothing is ever absolutely forgotten, once it has been impressed upon the mind. No impression, once recorded, ever ceases to exist. It is not lost, but merely becomes obscure and exists outside of the field of consciousness, to which however it may be recalled long afterward by some act of the will, or some association, according to the circumstances of the case. It is true that many impressions are never revived, either by volitional effort or involuntarily through association, but the impression is still there and its influence is manifest in our act and thoughts. If we could reach the depths of the subconscious mentality, we would find there every impression ever received by the mind—records of every thought that had ever been born to us—the memory of every act of our life. All these things would be there—unseen but exerting a subtle influence over us. We are what we are today, because of what we thought, said, saw, heard, felt and did yesterday. Man is a composite of his yesterdays. There is not a single thought or act or impression of our past life that has not had its influence in fixing our present intellectual and moral condition. Our opinion and thoughts today are largely the result of a long succession of little experiences of the past, long since forgotten, perhaps never to be recalled.

In other chapters of this book, we will take up the subject of training the subconscious faculties, to carefully store away, to remember the location of what they take in charge, and to quickly find and bring forth, at the behest of the Will, the desired thing. We will see that the memory is capable of infinite improvement, training and culture. When we realize that nothing is absolutely "forgotten," we begin to see the great possibilities in the direction of improvement in the art of receiving impressions, storing them away, and recalling them. We will see that the more clearly we impress upon the subconscious mentality, the more carefully we store away that impression, the more easily will we be able to bring it again into the field of consciousness. And we will see how wonderfully the subconscious workers may be trained to seek and find that which we want—how we may direct them as we would any others subject to our orders.

CHAPTER II.

ATTENTION AND CONCENTRATION.

Treating of the law of psychology that the intensity of the original impression determines the degree of future remembrance or recollection, and that the intensity of the original impression is proportionate to the attention given the subject or object producing the impression—Showing how the subconscious mentality stores away the impressions received, and how those which are carefully stored away may be more easily found and brought into the field of consciousness. Examples and illustrations are given, and the matter of attention, interest and concentration is discussed in their relation to Memory Culture.

It is a láw of psychology that the intensity of the original impression determines the degree of the future remembrance or recollection, and that the intensity of the impression is proportionate to the attention given the subject or object producing the impression. The experiences which leave the most permanent and intense impress upon the mind are those upon which the highest degree of attention has been bestowed. Some authorities go still further and hold that attention to the matter in hand is the most important intellectual habit possible to man, and that every man has within him the power to develop a certain degree of genius by developing the power of concentrated attention, which power is capable of almost infinite augmentation by resolute practice. It has been said that it is the different degrees of attention, rather than any difference in the abstract power of reasoning which constitutes the great differences noticeable between the minds of different individuals, and that attention constitutes the better half of all intellectual power.

The subconscious part of the mind stores away all impressions received through the senses, whether or not attention is bestowed upon the subject or object, but as such impressions are not ordinarily subject to conscious recall through the memory, they are of very little use to us in the field of consciousness, and for this purpose are practically as if they did not exist. So, for our purpose, we may assume that without at least some degree of attention no durable impression is stored way. In this sense we may say that it is not sufficient that an object transmit an impression through the avenue of the senses to the brain, but that in order that a thing be remembered attention and consciousness are necessary at the time of the primary impression.

To illustrate the difference between conscious attention and the mere receiving of impressions through the senses, let us imagine ourselves in a busy street in Chicago. Thousands of objects present themselves to our vision—thousands of sounds are transmitted to our brain through our organs of hearing—our sense of smell is receiving impressions—our sense of feeling is likewise doing its work as persons are coming in contact with us or we are brushing up against objects. In the midst of this confusion of sights, sounds, smells, feelings—with every avenue of sense impression open and receiving such impressions, we may be intently occupied with one particular sight, one sound, or even a thought—and all else that is going on around us is as if it were not. And all that we can readily remember of that particular moment is the one thing at which we were intently gazing—the one thing to which we were intently listening—or the particular thought occupying our mind at the moment.

A great proportion of the things we see, hear and feel, are almost immediately forgotten, because we have given them but a trifling degree of attention. It is said that poor memory is practically poor attention, and that the habit of careless observation is the twin of deficient memory. We refer to this phase of the subject in other parts of this book, and give instruction and exercises for the cultivation and development of the attention.

There have been differences of opinion regarding the question of whether or not one can give his attention to more than one object at the same time. The best authorities now seem to agree that the mind can actually attend to but one thing at a time, but it is able to move from one object to another, to and fro, with wonderful rapidity, which leads one to suppose that he has been directing his attention to two or more objects at the same time. Some very busy men are credited with the ability to do two or more things at the same time, but it is held that these men have simply developed an ability to glance from one thing to another with the greatest rapidity. Granville, speaking of this practice, say that it is "a sort of mental trapeze-flying, wherein the performer often gets an ugly fall, and may be permanently disabled." Bain sums up the matter when he says: "The fact never to be forgotten is that the human mind can attend to only one thing at a time, although it may shift the attention very rapidly, and thus overtake two or more things by turn."

When the mind is concentrated upon one subject or object, it is often oblivious to other sights and sounds which ordinarily would attract its momentary attention. Thus one who is engrossed in some particular thing may be oblivious to persons passing through the room, or to the striking of a clock within a few feet of him. The writer has noticed scores of people reading in the Chicago Public Library, apparently oblivious to sights or sounds or the passage of time. They would be so engrossed in their books that others might take, or rise from, seats beside them, and they would not notice it, and would not realize that it was closing time until politely tapped on the shoulder and asked to vacate their chair. We have known persons to be so engrossed in "day-dreams" that they would ride several stations past their destination on the elevated railroad or train. In the midst of battle, wounds are frequently unfelt for the time being. It is related of Henry Clay that wishing to speak on an important subject but a short time, he requested a fellow member to stop him at the expiration of the time fixed. He became so much engrossed in his speech that his friend could not get his attention, although at last, in desperation, he pushed a large pin in Clay's leg, several times. Clay paid no attention to the pin prick, but continued his speech for a long time after, and felt no sensation of pain although the pin drew blood. He stated afterwards that he was not conscious in the slightest degree to the friend's attempts to attract his attention, and, in fact, severely rebuked the friend for inattention to his request. It is said that a noted French writer became engrossed in his work on the morning of the massacre of St. Bartholemew, and was totally unaware of the carnage going on under his window. It is related that an Italian scientist became intensely interested in his experiments, and was not conscious of the battle going on in the streets of the town, and when at nightfall he emerged he was amazed to find Napoleon's troops occupying the city, and that the Austrian troops had vacated possession. It is said that Socrates once volunteered for a campaign, but becoming engrossed in a philosophical speculation, he stopped still and continued in a standing position for hours, and when he had solved the problem he found himself standing alone in the plain and the entire army several hour's march away from him.

If one wishes to devote his closest attention to a subject, he should, if possible, choose a time and place where and when his mind will be free from outside impressions. If you desire to interest a friend in an important matter, you would not seek him when he was occupied with other things, and would never dream of submitting the matter to his attention when he was in the midst of other business. You would wait until you could find him comparatively free from other interests, feeling sure that you would then get an attentive hearing. It is only men who have developed the power of concentrated attention who can drop one subject entirely for the moment, and give their undivided attention to a new subject. Of course, the memory follows the attention, and those things are best remembered of which the impressions are received when the mind is at ease and not otherwise employed.

Undivided attention will give remarkably clear impressions, and vastly increases the power of the faculties and gives them a strength which they ordinarily would not possess. A pain becomes more noticeable when the attention is directed toward it. It has been noticed that when the attention is firmly directed to any particular portion of the body, a sensation is often experienced at the part. And it is now conceded that the circulation can be increased in any organ and part of the body by increased attention directed there. If we wish to obtain the fullest and clearest impressions of an object or subject, we should concentrate our attention upon it. Concentration can, of course, be greatly increased by intelligent practice.

Men of great intellectual power are noted for their developed power of attention, and on the other hand, imbeciles and idiots are almost destitute of concentrated attention. The great man's mind, consequently, is stored full of strong, intense impressions, which he brings into the field of consciousness in his everyday work, while the man of deficient attention has but a small stock upon which to draw, and he consequently fails to manifest force and resourcefulness.

What we know about things is simply what we remember about them. This being so, one's knowledge is dependent entirely upon his memory. And as his memory is dependent upon his attention, then attention is the prime factor of knowledge. It will pay any man or woman to develop his or her power of attention. Learn to do one thing at a time, and to do that thing the best you know how. By giving a thing our attention and interest, the task or study will become pleasant and we will be able to do it well. And we will learn all that is to be learned about it. And we will remember what we have learned. Well has Chesterfield said: "There is time enough for everything in the course of a day, if we do but one thing at a time; but there is not enough time in a year if you try to do two things at a time." And Lord Burleigh backs him up, saying: "The shortest way of doing many things is to do one thing at a time." When we are attending to business, let us attend to it; when we are taking our rest or play, let us not allow a thought of business to enter. Let us love business at the office—let us loathe it at home.

Apparently opposed to the above theory of concentrated attention is the fact that many persons are able to do their best thinking when engaged in some light occupation such as light sewing, knitting, cutting the leaves of a book, looking idly at pictures, smoking, etc., but this apparent exception only proves the rule, the explanation being that the attention wandering from the main thought falls naturally upon the lighter occupation which makes only a minimum demand upon it, and which consequently does not distract the attention to any extent from the main point. The lighter task, in fact, may give the mind a little rest between thoughts. Therefore, if you find it difficult to concentrate your attention upon the subject or object before you, it may help you to take up some light task at the same time. But let the "side" task be light, as any important side issue would invariably divide the attention.

In studying the subject or object we may get the best results by directing the attention to the various details in succession, rather than by giving our attention to the thing as a whole. We get the best impression of a thing by our powers of analyzing and abstraction. We can make but little progress in intellectual work without exercising this power of analysis. We can best know a thing as a whole by knowing its parts separately. As Dr. Hering says: "Specialization is the mother of proficiency." Before one can learn and perform a complicated motion, he must first learn to perform each component part of that motion. When he knows how to perform each part, he knows how to perform the whole. And the same principle applies to intellectual perception and acquisition of impressions.

To those who have not been in the habit of concentrating or placing the attention firmly upon an object or subject, the task of forming the new habit will prove difficult and tiresome. But practice will make perfect, and after a time it will be found that the attention will be directed almost automatically, and without effort. All of the desirable qualities of the mind, referred to in these chapters, may be so developed by practice that they will almost unconsciously manifest when needed. Concentrated attention will be given when the subject demands it. Mental analysis likewise. Once establish a mental habit, and the mind will thereafter follow it. Clear away a mental path, and the mind will thenceforth travel it. The secret of attainment in Mental Development is PRACTICE and gradual improvement.

CHAPTER III.

ACQUIRING IMPRESSIONS.

Treating of the laws governing the acquiring of impressions—How impressions may be clearly received and retained—The difference between voluntary attention and involuntary attention—How sense impressions are received—How the senses may be trained to readily receive and store away impressions—The necessity of careful observation, etc., etc., etc.—Numerous illustrations are given showing the wonderful degree of perception, observation and memory attained by persons in all ages and countries, by careful and intelligent practice—Remarkable instances and interesting anecdotes are given to illustrate the subject discussed in this chapter.

As we have explained in a preceding chapter, the subconscious function of the mind receives every impression presented to it, and stores it away in its enormous storehouse. But there is a very great difference in the nature of the impressions received. Some are very vivid and strong; others fairly so; and others very faint and indistinct. The strength of the impression depends upon the interest bestowed upon it by the mind at the time of its occurrence, and the amount of voluntary attention bestowed upon it. A thing of interest, or a thing to which one has given attention, registers an impression much stronger than one exciting little or no interest or attention, and the record is much more easily recalled when it is needed.

Adhering to our illustration of the sub-conscious store-house, we may say that the attention given to a thing reaching the mind through the medium of the senses determines the size and shape of the thing to be stored away. And the interest awakened at the time of the impression gives the color to the impression. Remember this: The attention determines the size; the interest determines the color.

When one wishes to bring to light an article stored away in the storehouse, he finds it much easier to find a large article than a small one—much easier to locate one of a fiery red color than one of a neutral tint. This is true whether the goods are stored away carefully and systematically, or carelessly and without order. The careful and orderly keeping of stock, of course, greatly facilitates the finding of a desired article, but the size and color make the thing itself more conspicuous.

Frequent recalling or handling the article not only tends to acquaint the storekeeper with the location of the article, but also adds to its size and color, as each time it is brought out, a certain amount of attention and interest is bestowed upon it. Attention has been defined as "the focusing of consciousness." Consciousness may spread itself over a number of objects, just as the sun spreads its rays over countless things, or it may be focused upon a particular object, just as the rays of the sun may be concentrated, by the means of a glass, upon a single point. It is readily seen that the degree of attention is the measure of the impression made upon our sub-conscious mentality.

Attention has been divided by psychologists into two classes, i. e., involuntary and voluntary. The involuntary attention is that which is focused with a minimum of effort, or with apparently no effort at all on the part of the Will. Voluntary attention is that which is focused by an effort of the Will. The lower animals and undeveloped man have little or no voluntary attention, but the involuntary attention is there in full force. Developed man manifests a high degree of voluntary attention, the faculty of developing the same seeming to be one of the great differences between Man and the lower animals, the degree of voluntary attention indicating the stage of development of the man. Many men scarcely progress further than the border line of voluntary attention.

Involuntary attention is the birthright of the lower animal and man, in varying degrees. Voluntary attention is the result of development of the Will. In the lower animals, young children and undeveloped man, an object must be interesting to hold the attention for more than a moment. The developed man is able by an effort of the Will to direct his attention to an uninteresting object, and hold it there until he has conveyed to his mind the desired information regarding it. And he, likewise, is able to turn his attention from a most interesting object to one that is dull and uninteresting, all by the power of his Will. It is true that the developed man finds something of interest in nearly every object or subject, which renders it far easier to focus the attention than it would be in the case of the undeveloped man who sees nothing of interest in the same object or subject. The developed man also has the faculty of shutting out unwelcome subjects and objects from his attention—his field of consciousness. He uses his Will to accomplish this result, the process being similar to that by which he focuses his attention upon an uninteresting object or subject. The undeveloped man, having scarcely any voluntary attention, is almost at the mercy of outside impressions, and is practically in the position of the child who, viewing the passing circus parade, forgets himself, home and parents for the time being, and follows the procession until he is lost.

Impressions are received through the medium of the five senses. The senses may be divided into two classes, Direct and Indirect. The Direct senses are those conveying impressions to the brain direct, and are severally known as Feeling, Tasting and Smelling. In the exercise of these senses the person comes in contact with the object producing the impression, the contact being apparent in the case of Feeling and Tasting and less apparent, but none the less real, in the case of Smelling, in which case the minute particles emanating from the object come in contact with the olfactory nerves. The Indirect senses are those conveying impressions to the brain indirectly, and are known as Seeing and Hearing, in which cases the impression reaches the brain through the medium of light and sound waves, respectively.

The impressions conveyed by the Direct senses are not readily recalled by the memory, while those obtained by the Indirect senses are readily recalled, and a very high degree attained by intelligent practice. For instance, one cannot easily recall the precise taste, smell, or feel of an object, although he can distinctly recall the act and time of the tasting, smelling and feeling, and all the circumstances connected with it. But the mind indelibly registers the impression of the tasting, smelling and feeling so that it may be recognized when it again occurs. This faculty of recognition may be highly cultivated or developed, as in the cases of tea-tasters, wine experts, wool sorters, etc., in which instances the senses of Tasting, Smelling and Feeling are highly developed, and the memory of previous impressions readily recalled in its most minute details the instant the new impression reaches the brain. But it is difficult to recall the former impression of Tasting, Smelling or Feeling by an effort of the imagination so that it appears real. Exceptions are quoted by some writers who speak of certain gourmands, epicures, wine experts, etc., who can by an effort of the imagination and memory bring to their minds the distinct impression of the taste of their favorite dish or wine. Hypnotic subjects also seem to get such impressions by suggestion. But, generally speaking, it is hard to imagine a taste, smell or touch, as one does a sight or a sound.

But no difficulty of this kind is experienced in the case of impressions received through the senses of Seeing or Hearing, as one can not only recall the occurrences but can also readily picture the sight, or hear the sound, by means of the imagination aided by the memory. Some have this faculty largely developed, and can in the mind picture a sight or hear sounds almost as distinctly as in the original instance. Artists and musicians are examples of this fact.

It will readily be seen that in Memory Culture the acquiring of clear and distinct impressions is a most important feature. Unless there is something to recollect, there is no use for the memory. When you recall our illustration of the mental storehouse, with its varied and assorted stock of all sizes, shapes and colors, you will readily see the importance of having your mental packages and parcels of such size, shape and color as to to be easily seen and located when you need them.

Not only must the senses be trained to quickly and clearly record the impressions from outside so that they may be readily recalled, but the mind must be trained to direct its attention and interest to its own workings, to the end that thoughts and mental processes may be remembered when needed. Acquirement of impressions is often along two or more lines. For instance, in reading a printed page the eye records the impression of the words, sentences, paragraphs and page, while at the same time the other faculties of the mind receive the impression of the thought and meaning of the author; the impression of the thought and ideas of the reader; the conclusion arrived at by the reader after digesting and assimilating the reasoning of the author, mingling the same with the knowledge, information and opinions already stored away in his own mind. And all of these impressions may be recalled by means of the memory, according to the measure of the development of the faculty of memory in the particular individual.

Cultivation of Attention and Interest has produced almost marvelous results in many well known cases, and anyone may with a little practice acquire proficiency along these lines that will be as surprising to himself as amazing to his friends.

Robert Houdin, the celebrated French conjurer, whose best tricks depended materially upon his quick and correct observation, and his wonderful memory, had developed his faculty of rapid observation and attention as well as his memory, by years of careful practice. It is related of him that in his earlier days he would pass rapidly by a Paris shop, giving one sharp, quick glance at the window, then turning his eyes in another direction. Walking along for a few minutes he would stop and with pencil and paper endeavor to recall and describe as many articles as possible. He found that steady practice so sharpened his faculty of attention and observation that each day he would recollect a greater number of objects displayed in the windows, the explanation being that he was steadily developing the faculties which received and stored away impressions, as well as those which recalled them. It is said that in time he was able to rush past a large store window, filled with small wares, and receive such a full, clear and sharp impression of the objects displayed that he could, hours afterward, recall and describe every article with scarcely a mistake. This development made Houdin what he was, and helped him to amass a fortune. His mind apparently became like a photographic plate, and registered everything in range, and all he had to do was to recall the impression and call off the names of the objects as he saw them with his mind's eye.

Rudyard Kipling, in his delightful story, "Kim," describes a similar proceeding. The old teacher Lurgan Sahib was training the boy for the Secret Service, in which the quick and clear seeing of things meant success, and perhaps even life itself. The old man took from a drawer a handful of jewels, gems, etc., and bids Kim to gaze upon them as long as he desired, and then see what he could remember of what he had seen. A native boy, who had been trained in this way for some time, is also there. Kim bent over the tray and gazed at the fifteen jewels upon it. He thought it was an easy game. The tray was then covered, and the native boy hastily scribbled his recollection on a sheet of paper. " 'There are under that paper five blue stones, one big, one smaller, and three small,' said Kim, all in haste. 'There are four green stones and one with a hole in it; there is one yellow stone that I can see through, and one like a pipe-stem. There are two red stones, and—and—I made the count fifteen, but two I have forgotten. No! give me time. One was of ivory, little and brownish, and—and—give me time.' " But Kim could do no better. " 'Hear my count,' cried the native child, 'First are two flawed sapphires, one of two ruttees and one of four, as I should judge. The four ruttee sapphire is chipped at the edge. There is one Turkestan turquoise, plain with green veins, and there are two inscribed—one with the name of God in gilt, and the other being cracked across, for it came out of an old ring, I cannot read. We have now the five blue stones; four flamed emeralds there are, but one is drilled in two places, and one is a little carven.' 'Their weight,' said Lurgan Sahib, impassively. 'Three—five—five and four ruttees, as I judge it. There is one piece of old greenish amber, and a cheap cut topaz from Europe. There is one ruby of Burma, one of two ruttees, without a flaw. And there is a ballas ruby, flawed, of two ruttees. There is a carved ivory from China, representing a rat sucking an egg; and there is last—Ah— ha!—a ball of crystal as big as a bean set in gold leaf!' He clapped his hands at the close." Kim feels much mortified at the superiority of the native boy. "'But how is it done?' asked Kim. 'By doing it many times over till it is done perfectly—for it is worth doing." I advise you to read this book (and it is full of good things), and see how Kim profited by the instructions of the old master. This game so graphically portrayed by that master of description, Kipling, is a favorite with the Orientals, many of whom attain a great proficiency in it as did Houdin in his form of the same game. And any of you may do the same, if you will take the time and trouble to acquire the "knack."

It is related of a well-known artist that at a first sitting of a patron he would often sit gazing at his sitter for an hour at a time, and would then dismiss him, telling him that he need not return. He would then work at the portrait for months without another sitting, gazing from time to time at the empty chair of his late sitter, and then reproducing his features on the canvas. He said that he could actually *see* his model in the chair. the impression having apparently been indelibly impressed upon his memory. This, of course, is an extreme example, but other artists have developed the same faculty to a scarcely less wonderful degree.

The Chinese have a different letter or word-sign for every word, and the Chinese scholar carries thousands of these word-signs in his mind, without any trouble. Our own children are doing the same thing on a smaller scale by reason of the new system of reading now in vogue in our schools. When we, their parents, learned to read we would first begin to spell the word before we could read it, and it was a long time before we reached "Con-stan-ti-no-ple," but now our little ones are taught the shape or general appearance of the word, instead of its separate letters or sound, and to them "Constantinople" is as easy to *read* as "Cat" (and "Cat" as hard to *spell* as "Constantinople," sometimes).

Similar results are recorded of musicians, many of whom have been able to reproduce page after page of music they had heard but once or twice. A celebrated composer, while but a boy, is said to have listened to a celebrated Mass sung at a monastery. the scorce of which was religiously guarded by the monks. Upon his return to his room he reproduced the entire Mass on paper, without the mistake of a single note. The monks forgave the theft in their admiration of the remarkable feat. Lesser feats of memorizing music are not uncommon. And mind you, it is not alone the faculty of memory that renders these things possible, but the developed faculty of *seeing* and *hearing* things clearly and distinctly.

There are Jews living to-day who can repeat by heart, from any given word, the whole of the Talmud, which is a library in itself. Leland tells a tale of a Hindu who did not understand English at all, who having fifty lines of "Paradise Lost" read to him, repeated it accurately from sound, and then rehearsed it backwards. In earlier times, when books were costly, men were dependent upon their memories, and many developed memories which would now be regarded as marvelous, but which were then quite the ordinary thing, possessed by all who made any pretense to study. In the thirteenth and fourteenth centuries, students flocked to the universities in thousands. Books were scarce and costly, and the ancient custom of committing whole works to memory still prevailed. Schliemann, in his *Ilios,* tells us that his memory was bad originally, but he so perfected it by an indomitable will and hard work, that at last he learned a new language every six months, so as to write and speak it perfectly. And all this while he was making a fortune in the wholesale grocery business.

Japanese children pass at least two years in studying mere letters or signs before they begin to read. This is much harder than anything known in our schools, and involves the exercise of memory only. This training has given the Japanese wonderful memories. One of their writers, Hirata Atsutane, compiled a great work on the myths and legends of his country, and is said to have composed the first three volumes of the text and several volumes of the introduction, without referring to a single book from which he had drawn his information.

Grotius and Pascal are said to have forgotten nothing that they had ever read or thought. Cardinal Mezzofanti, who is said to have mastered over a hundred different languages, declared that he never forgot a word that he had once learned. There is a story on record of an old village grave-digger who could remember the day of every funeral in the churchyard for thirty-five years, the age of the deceased, and the names of those attending the funeral.

Seneca was able to repeat two thousand disconnected words after having heard them once, in the same order as they were given, simply by his natural powers of memory. His friend, Porteus Latio, never forgot any of the speeches he had ever delivered, and never found his memory fail for a single word. Cyneas, an ambassador to the Romans from King Pyrrhus, learned in a single day the names of the assembled people so well that the next day he was able to salute the senate and the populace, each by his own name. Pliny says that Cyrus knew the name of every soldier in his army. Francis Luarez could repeat all of St. Augustine's works, making quotations and citing the number of the page and the line where they could be found. Themistocles could call by their names the 20,000 citizens of Athens. Muretus tells of a young Corsican pupil who could repeat backward and forward 36,000 unconnected words, after having heard them but once. He said that he could do better, but the men who were reading to him became exhausted. There came to this Corsican a young man whose memory was wretched. The Corsican instructed him with such success that in a week or two the pupil could repeat five hundred words, backward and forward.

Magliabechi, the great Florentine bibliophile, had a wonderful memory for books and libraries. He knew the location, shelf, and number of every book in his own great library, and of the other great libraries of the world. Once the Grand Duke of Tuscany asked him where he could find a copy of a certain rare book, and he replied that there was only one copy in existence, and that copy was "in the library of the Grand Seignior, in Constantinople, on the seventh shelf of the third case to the right as you enter." Joseph Scaliger committed to memory the Iliad and Odyssey, in less than a month, and in three months had mastered the entire list of the Greek poets, and committed them to memory. This man is said to have often complained of his poor memory!

By practice one may develop the power of concentration and attention as applied to thoughts as well as other things. The same rule and reason maintains in each case. In subsequent chapters we will take up this phase of the subject. But our attention will first be directed to the development of the faculty of acquiring impressions through the senses of Seeing and Hearing.

CHAPTER IV.

EYE PERCEPTION AND MEMORY.

Treating of the receiving of impressions through the sense of sight—The vital importance of the training of the eye to receive impressions clearly and distinctly—The benefit of such training in every day and business life—The importance of such training in Memory Culture—Showing that the majority of people "look at" rather than "see" things—Interesting examples and illustrations are given, showing how this faculty has been developed by those who have devoted attention to the subject, and the general rules governing the development and cultivation of this faculty of the mind are given.

It has been well said that "the eyes are the windows of the soul," and it is indeed true that through these windows the mind receives the greatest number of impressions, and those impressions of the very finest quality. And it will be noticed that the subject of Memory Culture is perhaps more closely allied to the training of the mind to correctly register the impressions received through the medium of the eye than the cultivation of any other of the senses.

We can scarcely too strongly urge upon our readers the vital importance of the training of the Eye to receive correct impressions clearly and distinctly. Such training, and the consequent development, will result to the benefit of the man or woman in any walk of life; in any profession, business or trade. It is not merely the artist or sculptor who needs the aid of the trained eye, but every artisan, business man, or professional man who has not developed along these lines, suffers every day for his negligence.

The artist cannot reproduce unless he observes correctly; the writer cannot describe scenes, persons or character unless he has the sharpened faculty of observation; the artisan needs no one to tell him of the importance of seeing things. There is no occupation the followers of which are not benefited by trained power of observation.

One adds very materially to his fund of information, and to his pleasure by cultivating the art of perception. In traveling, for instance, many persons miss much of the best scenery—many objects of the greatest interest—by failing to perceive them. They return and read works of travel describing the same location, and are astonished at the wealth of description while they saw so little. And many miss the best parts of a book, by reason of careless reading.

The Indian and the backwoodsman will notice the broken twig, the turned leaf, the footprint, where the untrained observer sees nothing uncommon.

We remember reading somewhere of a merchant who was laughed at for having an ignorant man in his employ as buyer. He replied that it was true that the employee spelled worse than Josh Billings—that his grammar was enough to make Lindley Murray turn over in his grave—that he had never read the works of a standard author—but he knew how to SEE things—he bought thousands of dollars' worth of goods every year for the merchant and had never been known to make a mistake, or to fail to note a defect, or any objectionable feature in the goods. This man had cultivated the faculty of perception, and was turning it to account.

Very few of us notice the details of the most common objects. How many of you know whether a cow's ears are above, below, behind or in front of her horns? How many can tell whether a cat descends from a tree head or tail first. How many know whether cows and horses rise with their fore or hind feet first, or whether both animals have the same habit of rising? How many know how the number "four" appears on a watch dial?—most of you will say IV—look at your watch.

The eminent scientist Agassiz had a wonderful success in training his pupils to observe. The highly trained powers of perception which he developed in them undoubtedly contributed largely to the success of the large number of his pupils who made names and places for themselves in after years. It is related of him that one day a favorite pupil asked for additional training along these lines. Agassiz handed him a jar containing a fish, and told him to carefully examine it and report to him later what he had noticed about the fish. The pupil had seen the same kind of fish before, and could not understand why the professor had given him so trifling a task. He looked at the specimen but saw nothing of interest. He was unable to find the professor, and was compelled to remain with the tiresome fish for several hours, much to his disgust. After a bit, to relieve the monotony, he took the fish out of the jar and began to draw its figure. This was easy enough until he began to fill in the details. Then he made the interesting discovery that the fish had no eyelids, also several little points of interest that were new to him.

When Agassiz returned he seemed disappointed that the student had found out so little about the fish, and told him to try for a few hours more. The student, finding that there was no escape, started to work in earnest, bearing in mind Agassiz's remark that "a pencil is the best of eyes." He began to see more and more of interest in that fish, and grew quite interested in the task. The professor would come in from time to time, and hear of the student's new discoveries, but would say little or nothing. He kept the student at work on that same fish for three long days, and the student wondered greatly that he had been able to see so little before, where there was so much to be seen and noted. The student, many years after, had made a name for himself, and was wont to tell this story, with the observation that the lesson gained by the study of that fish had extended to the details of every subsequent study, and that the experience thus gained was of inestimable value to him. It is said of Agassiz that he could deliver a popular lecture on an insect like the grasshopper, and make it so interesting that the audience became as intent as if they were witnessing a play.

In London there are said to be places where young thieves are instructed in the art of rapid and close observation. The "professor" instructing young rascals will place in his hand a number of small objects, such as a key, a button, a coin, a ring, etc. He will open his hand an instant before his class, who are required not only to name the objects seen but to describe them. Then changes will be made in the object and the boys must detect the article substituted at once. These students, after a course of training, are sent out as beggars. They endeavor to catch a glimpse into offices, rooms, houses, etc., and to note any article of value within range of their sight, its location, the doors, locks, etc., etc. They report to headquarters and if the prospects are good a burglary is forthcoming.

The above will be seen to resemble the method used to train "Kim," as related in a preceding chapter. Readers of Conan Doyle's fascinating "Sherlock Holmes" tales will remember the wonderful powers of perception possessed by that amateur detective, and the results accomplished because of same. Gamblers are close observers, and can often tell the hand held by their opponent, by the expression of his face, although the opponent may not be aware of betraying himself.

The Italians have a game called Morra, which is a great favorite among their boys, and which when played regularly makes the little chaps as observant as foxes. It is played by two boys, and consists in both throwing out any number of fingers simultaneously, each player crying out as rapidly as he can the number of fingers shown by the other. We have noticed a variation of this game, played by the Italian newsboys in Chicago, while waiting for their papers. One will wait until he has the attention of the other boy, and then will suddenly throw out his fist with one or more fingers displayed, shouting "Morra." The other boy must name the number of fingers immediately, else he will receive over the head a sound whack from a rolled up newspaper in the hand of the other boy. Coture, the great teacher of drawing, instructed his pupils to let their eyes rest for a moment on passers-by in the street, and then attempt to draw them. The plan met with perfect success, after practice. At first only a hat, or an arm or a leg would be distinctly registered, but in a short time the entire figure in all its details was recorded. In the School of Design in St. Petersburg, Russia, the pupils are instructed to study an object for ten minutes, and then, the object being withdrawn, they proceed to draw it. Varney, the celebrated teacher, would place the object to be drawn in one room, and have his pupils at work in another room, allowing them to go from time to time to take a look at the object.

Garbielli, a French artist, painted a most expressive portrait of James Gordon Bennett, whom he had only seen once as he went by rapidly in a carriage. One of the most speaking pictures of Lincoln we have ever seen was painted by a talented but practically unknown artist in New Jersey, who was a most ardent admirer of the great President, whom he had seen but once. The artist was so overcome with emotion at hearing of the assassination of his idol that he sought his easel for solace, and reproduced the murdered President's features entirely from memory. Many years ago, about 1845, the old Academy of Fine Arts in Philadelphia, was destroyed by fire, and among other valuable paintings there perished a picture by Murillo, entitled "The Roman Daughter." Nearly thirty-five years afterwards, Sartain drew the picture from memory. In 1805 the French troops carried away a masterpiece of Rubens, which had formed the altar-piece in the Church of St. Peter, in Cologne. A local painter, a great admirer of the picture, made from memory a copy of the painting which seems to be absolutely perfect in drawing, detail and color. The original painting was afterwards restored and the copy compared with it, but the closest inspection fails to show any perceptible difference between them. There is a waiter in a leading hotel in a large city, who takes the hats from the guests as they enter the dining room. He can identify the owners of hundreds of hats, without a single mistake, by associating the face of the wearer with the hat, and recalling it by eye memory. "I put the face under the hat, and then I know whose hat it is," he says, and as each guest leaves the room he is handed his own hat. Many hotel-keepers remember the names of thousands of guests.

A story is told of Stevens, formerly a police official of New York, to the effect that he wished to ascertain the character of a man who occupied a room which he kept closed against all intruders. One day Stevens knocked, and the door was opened but a few inches for an instant. Stevens' keen eye, in that instant, took in all the contents of the room. He saw hanging around suits of clothes of all kinds, and he recognized among them certain suits that had been worn as disguises by a man he "wanted." An arrest followed, and the man proved to be a noted criminal for whom the police of the continent were searching. A noted police official of London instructs new men on his force to look on both sides of them as they walk down a crowded street, he having noticed that the average man looks chiefly upon the right hand.

The eye, of course, transmits to the brain every ray of light entering it, and it is believed that every impression as received is registered faintly. But the mind fails to store away and subsequently recall any impressions except those which are the result of more or less interest or attention. But we may so train the sense of seeing that the impressions are received so clearly and distinctly that the mind considers it worth while to store them away carefully that they may be recalled when needed, instead of dumping them in a pile in the waste heap where it is almost impossible to find them when one desires them.

Very few people are close observers. The average person will remember a thing in a general way—will recall what it is like—but the details are missing. A thing of interest, however, receives a greater share of the attention, and a clear and full impression is registered. An instance of the operation of interest in this connection is had in the example of an average man and woman walking leisurely along the street. Another woman passes them, wearing a rather attractive gown. Both notice her. The man remembers only the fact that "she had on something blue" and that "her sleeves bulged out near the wrist and she had on rather a big hat." If he remembers that much he has done well—many men would not have seen the sleeves, and the rest of the impression would have been hazy. But the woman would be able to tell just what the other woman had on—the waist and how it was trimmed—the style in sleeves to a fine detail; the skirt, how it was cut and of what material composed; its quality and probable cost; the hat and its feathers, silk and velvet; all the little points of style, etc. She would be able to describe to a woman friend all that she had seen, and the friend would be able to see it all "in her mind's eye." Now, both the man and the woman had equally good eyes—both received a photographic impression of the passing woman and her finery, and yet notice what a difference in the respective observation of the two people. What caused the difference? Simply the fact that the woman's interest was along the lines of dress, and she had trained her attention to focus on such things. With the man there was no interest—no attention. And yet the man probably remembered that the woman had bright blue eyes and fluffy golden hair—that is, if he were a young man.

But the quality of interest may be trained and acquired, and the quality of attention will follow it.

You, of course, realize that it is not the eye that requires training, for every healthy eye does its work well. It is that part of the mind that "sees" through the eye that needs the lessons you are about to give it. The eye is the camera—the mind the sensitive plate. You wish to develop the faculty of observation. Your desire gives you an interest in the subject, and in the details of the plan, and you devote your attention to it. Important factors these—Interest and Attention—don't forget them. But the mind has been lazy, and it will take time, patience and practice to get it down to work in earnest.

In order to remember objects, it is first necessary to see them plainly—to have the mind register a clear impression of them and store them away carefully as things of value. And the only way to get the mind to do this is to train its powers of observation. Things to be impressed upon the mind must be observed carefully and thoughtfully. This training of the powers of observation will amply repay the student for the time and labor expended, and the task itself is not irksome or dull, as the progress of the task is attended with such marked improvement of so pleasant a character that the student almost forgets that it is a task rather than a pleasant series of experiments.

In the next chapter we will give you a number of exercises calculated to develop your powers of observation—intended to help you to "see" things clearly and carefully. These exercises are useful not only in training your memory, but will give you such sharp powers of observation that you will be a much more valuable man to yourself and others than ever before. It will be a liberal education to you, along new lines.

CHAPTER V.

EXERCISES IN EYE PERCEPTION.

Treating of the means whereby the faculty of careful observation and clear-seeing may be developed and cultivated, to the end that the student may be able to receive and store away clear and distinct impressions of the things coming before his sight—Interesting and useful exercises are given to aid the student in "the art of seeing," which exercises, if carefully practiced, will develop the faculty of observation to a wonderful extent, and will not only greatly improve the memory, but will make the student a careful observer and improve his general usefulness—The importance of the subject is not generally understood.

Exercise 1.

One of the simplest but best exercises in the training of the power of observation consists in the correct seeing of familiar objects. This may seem like a very easy thing, but after you have tried it a few times you will have more respect for it.

Begin by placing before you some familiar object (something of a bright color is preferable, as it is easier to remember bright objects). Suppose it is a book, an apple or inkstand. Look at it intently, calmly but deliberately, for a few moments, trying to get the picture impressed upon your mind. Then close your eyes, and try to remember as much as possible about the object. Try to remember its shape, its details. Fix these things in your mind. Then open your eyes and take another look, and see how many details you missed in your mental picture. Note these forgotten points carefully, then close the eyes again and endeavor to re-form the picture. Then open the eyes and take stock over again, repeating until you are able to form a perfect mental picture of the object in all its details. A little practice will give you a wonderful proficiency in this experiment which will prove quite gratifying to you. But it is not alone what you have gained in this experiment, but the preliminary training you have acquired for greater things, that renders it "worth while."

Exercise 2.

After you have mastered Exercise 1, take one of the same objects with which you have familiarized yourself, and, after getting a good mental impression of it, try to draw the general shape and such details as you remember, with a pencil upon a sheet of paper. Do not hesitate because you are not an artist. We are not trying to make an artist of you and wish but to develop your observation and the recalling of what you have observed. Take something easy for the first trial, and you will feel less discouraged. The success of your drawing will depend not upon its artistic merit, but upon the percentage of details, etc., you have been able to remember sufficiently well to indicate upon the paper. It is astonishing how these two exercises will develop your faculties of observation and recollection. After a bit you will be able to give one good look at a thing, and then make a rough drawing, showing all its principal points and details.

You, of course, understand that the drawing is not from the object direct, but from the mental picture of it. After you have noted all the details in your mental picture, take a look at the object and see what you have missed. Then repeat, as in Exercise 1. In both of these exercises, change your objects frequently, thus gaining proficiency and giving the mind an agreeable change.

Exercise 3.

Begin noticing the details of things, instead of observing only the thing in its general aspect. It has been said that intelligent observation was the most difficult of arts. Do not try to "take in" a complex object in its entirety at one look, at the start. This is something that is reserved for future practice when you have developed further. Take in the details of portions of the object; rivet these in your mind, and then proceed to the next portion, and so on.

Take faces for example. Nothing is more mortifying than to forget the faces of those whom we have met, and many a man's chances have been injured by a lack of correct observation in this direction. The trouble with most of us is that we have been endeavoring to remember faces, by observing them as a whole, paying no attention to details. Begin practicing on your acquaintances, then proceeding to strangers, and in a short time you will be surprised at your proficiency in recalling details of countenances. Notice carefully the nose, eyes, mouth, chin, color of hair, general shape of head, etc. You will find that you will be able to recall the nose of Smith, or the eyes of Brown, or the chin of Tompkins, and so on.

Before doing this, sit down and try to describe the features of some of your most intimate friends. You will be surprised at the scantiness of your recollection of them. You have never taken a good look at them, in detail. If this is so, how can you expect to remember the faces of strangers. Begin noticing everyone you meet, and studying features carefully, and then later on taking a pencil and endeavoring to jot down a brief description of their features. This exercise will prove very interesting, and you will notice your rapid improvement from the start.

Another good exercise along this line, is to observe the exterior of buildings, in detail. First try to describe some building you pass every day. You will be able to give a fair idea of its general aspect, its shape, color and so on. But how about the number of windows on each floor, the size and location of the doors, the shape of the roof, porch, chimneys, etc. How about the cornices, the trimmings, etc.? And the angles of the roof? You find that you have not really *seen* the house at all, do you not? You have merely looked *at* it. Begin now, noticing the buildings on your road, and then later in the day, endeavor to form a mental picture of the details, seeing how many you can remember of image correctly. Next day take the same building and look for new details (you'll find many of them) and keep this up until you know something about the building in question. This is a most valuable exercise for the training of the powers of observation.

Exercise 4.

We have mentioned the exercise whereby "Kim" was trained. We have also told you of how young thieves are trained by a similar exercise. This same course of training may be followed by the student, with great profit, and considerable amusement, the latter being particularly the case when two or more persons practice it together. In fact, all of these exercises may be made far more interesting if two or more persons practice them together, the friendly rivalry and keen interest thus aroused being calculated to stimulate the student and sharpen the powers of observation.

The following exercise game is interesting:. Place upon a table at least seven articles covered with a cloth. Remove the cloth and count *ten* slowly, then replace the cloth and have those taking part in the game describe the articles as fully as possible, writing down their descriptions. This can be varied by raising the cover and counting while one person alone is at the table, allowing him to retire to another part of the room to write down his impressions, while another is looking, and so on. The number of articles on the table may be increased, in time to fifty small articles. It is wonderful what a degree of proficiency in observation may be attained by some of the contestants in this manner. The tale of "Kim" and his task, while purely fiction, is certainly based upon some actual experience observed or known to Kipling, for such practices are quite common in India, a similar practice being observed by certain of the Yogis. And not only can those thus developed take part in a game of this kind, but their powers of observation become so sharpened that without effort they may see many things in their everyday life that others would not notice, and thus become quite valuable to the business with which they are connected.

In this same class of exercises, may be placed the experiment of Houdin, who walked past the store windows and then recalled the articles displayed in the windows passed. We have related this experiment in another chapter. This exercise may be practiced, as a change from the ones above mentioned. It adds variety, and also tends to develop the powers of observation and concentration while the observer is surrounded with the noises and sights of outside things. Many other exercises of this sort will suggest themselves to the student as he progresses, and he will find the subject very fascinating, after he once masters the "trick" of doing the thing.

Exercise 5.

We have seen a game played in the country which is an excellent means of developing the powers of observation. It is a little different from the exercises given above, inasmuch as the articles are moving and the attention must be rapidly focused upon them in order to get a clear impression. The game is played by having a person stand behind a screen or curtain, and tossing an object up in the air so that those in front of the screen may see it for a moment, above the screen, as it rapidly rises and falls. Those who have developed rapid perception will be able to describe the article with a wonderful degree of clearness and detail. Several things may be tossed up at one time, after the participants become proficient in the game.

Exercise 6.

An interesting exercise is the placing of a domino before the student, requiring him to name the sum total of the spots at once, instead of counting them in the ordinary way. Then try two dominos, then three, and so on. With a little practice one is enabled to give the sum total of the spots on several dominos almost instantaneously. A variation of this exercise, and one much easier to master, is to flash a playing card before the student, requiring him to name the color, suit and number of spots on the card. This may be done rather slowly at first, increasing the speed until the student barely catches a glimpse of the card as it passes before him.

Exercise 7.

Many persons are able to practically grasp the meaning of a paragraph of printed matter at a glance. Busy men who read newspapers have this faculty, and men and women employed in journalism are often able to grasp the sense of a page by apparently just glancing at it. Book reviewers also have this faculty. (In fact judging from the character of some of the reviews in the daily press, the reviewer does not look at the book at all.) The writer, in his editorial work, has to "go over" a mass of exchanges every month. At first this took much time, but at present a rapid turning over of leaves and a summing up of the contents of a page at a glance proves equally profitable, and he seems to almost "sense" an interesting article at first glance. It is all a matter of practice. Prof. Porter, of Yale, was said to have been able to read at a single glance nearly half a page of an ordinary text-book.

Begin by trying to read several words at a glance; then sentences; then several sentences; then a group of sentences; then paragraphs, and so on. In all this work of developing mental faculties, one must proceed as he would were he developing a muscle or set of muscles—by degrees.

Exercise 8.

A valuable exercise is that of taking mental stock of a room and its contents. Many women are able to do this without any instructions, but the powers of observation of most men are not great in this direction, so they should develop it. If you are a man and are studying these lessons with a woman she will be able to distance you in this exercise and probably most of the others. Many women seem to see *everything* that interests them, and many of them never forget what they have seen.

Go into a room and take a rapid survey of it and its contents, trying to get a good mental photograph of as many articles as possible—the size of the room, the height of the ceiling, the color of the paper, the number of doors and windows, the chairs, tables, carpet, pictures, etc. Then go out of the room and mark down what you have seen. Then compare with the room itself. Repeat until you have mastered the exercise. You will, by practice, be able to correctly describe any place you have visited, almost without effort, your powers of observation having automatically registered impressions, after you have trained them for a while.

Exercise 9.

At night, go over the affairs of the past day and endeavor to recollect and describe the things and persons with whom you have met and whom you have seen. It is surprising how little you will be able to recall at the start, and how much you will be able to recall after a little practice. This is not merely the ability to recall, but the ability to observe. Your subconscious mentality will recognize the necessity of noting things clearly and then placing them where they belong.

CHAPTER VI.

EAR PERCEPTION AND MEMORY.

Treating of the receiving of impressions through the sense of hearing—The advantages of cultivating this faculty—The rules governing same—Instances of wonderful ear perception and memory, etc., etc., etc.—This phase of the subject is one which usually receives but scant attention from students, and yet some of the most remarkable instances of memory development depended upon the cultivation and development of "ear attention"—For long ages, the religious, philosophical and legal teachings of ancient races were transmitted from mouth to ear, the memory performing feats now deemed almost incredible, but which may be reproduced by any one devoting sufficient attention to the subject.

We are in the habit of using the word perception as meaning the cognizing of something by the sense of sight, but the term is equally applicable to the cognizing or discerning of something through the medium of the sense of hearing. There is a great difference in individuals in matter of retaining impressions through these two senses. Some remember far more readily that which they see, while others find it much easier to recall a thing by the impression received from hearing. One man will remember an old acquaintance at once as soon as he sees him, while another will not recognize the face of the stranger, but will remember him at once when he speaks. We have known cases in which persons who had not been seen or heard of for years were recogniged by one-time friends by their voices, heard over the telephone. We remember a case reported in the daily papers of a detective failing to recognize a noted criminal through his wonderful disguise and "make-up," but who identified and arrested his man at once when the latter spoke, although it had been ten years or more since the detective had heard his voice. We have known men and women to recognize a former school mate whom they had not seen since childhood, simply by remembering the voice, although the childish treble had been replaced by the mature tones of the man or woman.

As a rule, impressions received through the eye are received more rapidly, but somehow the memory seems to hold better that which enters the mind by means of the ear. Many of us remember what we have heard, much more readily than that which we have read. Some writers hold, however, that in the case of remembering the words of lectures, etc., the ear is aided by the eye, in the direction of the remembrance of the appearance of the speaker, his gestures, expression, etc., and we are inclined to at least partially agree with this view. But the lecture seems to be much more "alive" when we hear it than when we afterwards read it in print. Perhaps the better plan is to both hear and then read the lecture or sermon, if possible, and thus get the benefit of both sense memories.

Musicians, of course, have trained their sense of hearing to a remarkable degree, and the musical ear can detect at once the slightest inharmony, or the most trifling variation from the proper note on the violin. But many others have also developed this faculty to a wonderful degree. Machinists can detect the slightest variation from the clear tone resulting from the tapping of a piece of machinery with a hammer. Railroad men can detect from the slight difference in the sound whether anything is the matter with the wheels or track while the train is running at a high rate of speed. Engineers will detect the slightest change in the song of the engines, and knowing that something is wrong somewhere will shut off the power at once. Old river pilots will recognize the sound of the whistle of any boat on the river, and the tones of the different church bells are recognized by residents of a large city. Telegraphers recognize the differnt styles of the various operators on their lines, and will detect the "style" of a new operator in a moment, merely from the almost imperceptible difference in the "tick" of the instrument.

In ages long since past, when written language was almost unknown, the knowledge and experience of one generation was passed along from father to son, from teacher to pupil, from mouth to ear. The utmost power of attention and concentration must have been employed by the hearer, for what was thus taught was retained and preserved intact and afterward delivered, in turn, to the son or pupil of the hearer. It is said that these students could repeat teaching of the greatest length without the omission or change of a single word. The poems of the ancient Greeks were thus passed along from generation to generation. Thus were the sagas of the Norsemen transmitted. And in like manner were the philosophies of ancient Persia and India handed down along the ages. The Oriental teachers distrusted stone and papyrus, and preferred that their sacred teachings be indelibly recorded in the brains of their pupils, and thus endure as a living truth.

It is related that, over two thousand years ago, a Chinese emperor became jealous of his ancestors and of the greatness of the past history of the nation. He sought to destroy all the historical, religious and philosophical records of the past, that in the future everything might date from his reign. He burned everything in the way of a written or graven record in the empire, including the works of Confucius. The past history of the empire was destroyed and lives to-day only in the shape of tradition, but the works of Confucius endure, intact, thanks to the wonderful power of memory possessed by an old Confucian sage, who had stored away in his mind the teachings received in his youth, and who managed to keep them hidden away until after the death of the iconoclastic Emperor, when he had the works of the great Chinese philosopher reproduced from his dictation. So perfect was his memory, that when, long years after, there was found an old Confucian manuscript, that had somehow escaped the fires of the former Emperor, it was found that the old sage had not missed a single word of the text. The Chinese of to-day have profited by this lesson, and writers say that if the Chinese classics were to be destroyed to-day, fully a million Chinamen could repeat them perfectly to-morrow, notwithstanding the fact that the feat would be almost equal to the reproducing of our Bible.

The same custom maintains in India, where, although they have manuscripts two thousand years old, they have scholars who have stored away in their minds the great philosophies which have been handed down from a time when writing was unknown to their race. Sanscrit is a dead language, but it has been passed down in the transmitting of these religious and philosophical teachings—not only the mere words, but the accent, inflection and pronunciation as well. It is said that many Hindu scholars can to-day repeat the Vedas, containing nearly one million words. It takes years to accomplish the task of committing this to memory, a few lines being learned every day, much rehearsing and reviewing being done. The lesson is taught entirely by word of mouth, no reference to manuscript being permitted.

The Kabala, or Secret Teaching, of the Jews was thus transmitted, and the religious teachings of the Druids are believed to have likewise been transmitted and preserved. The ancient Greeks and Romans were adepts in this form of memory, and instances are cited where citizens could repeat word for word every important speech they had heard.

According to Max Muller, the entire text and glossary of Panini's Sanscrit grammar were handed down orally for 350 years, before being committed to writing. This work alone is almost equal in size to the Bible. There are Hindu priests now living who can repeat accurately the entire poems of the Mahabarata, of 300,000 slokas or lines. The Slavonian minstrels of the present day have by heart immensely long epic poems. And the Algonquin Indians committed to memory and repeated accurately their sagas or mystic legends of almost interminable length. The ancient laws of Iceland were not written or printed, but were carried in the minds of the judges and lawyers of that land. And their sagas relate that the lawyers of that day were able to carry in their minds not only the laws themselves but also the innumerable number of precedents which had grown around the law.

Of course, there is no necessity for these feats of memory at the present time, but we do not doubt that if the necessity arose, modern men could soon duplicate the feats of the ancients.

Reading aloud will prove a great help in committing to memory that which is being read, and also in impressing upon the mind the meaning of the words. Longeve says: "Reading aloud gives a power of analysis which silent reading can never know. The eye runs over the page, skips tedious bits, glides over dangerous spots. But the ear hears everything. The ear makes no cuts. The ear is delicate, sensitive and clairvoyant to a degree inconceivable by the eye. A word which glanced at, passed unnoticed, assumes vast proportions when read aloud."

CHAPTER VII.

EXERCISES IN EAR PERCEPTION.

Treating of the development of ear perception and memory, following the preceding chapter, and giving numerous exercises designed to develop and cultivate the faculty of intelligent hearing—Instances of greatly developed ear perception show us that the majority of people have the sense of hearing but imperfectly developed, and place but little attention upon what they hear, and this faculty may be greatly developed and improved by intelligent practice—Good authorities have stated that "one-half of the deafness that exists is the result of inattention," and one-half of the poor memories are traceable to the same cause—The exercises are designed to remedy this defect—This chapter includes a valuable system for memorizing things heard, following the lines laid down by the ancient Hindu teachers when transmitting their sacred teachings.

It is rather more difficult to formulate a list of exercises for the development of ear perception than to give a similar list of exercises for the eye. The development of ear perception along the lines we have laid down for eye perception would lead us into a field of little practical benefit. We would be accused of teaching our pupils the art of mimicry or ventriloquism, in stead of memory training. The ventriloquist, as you are, of course, aware, will so correctly reproduce the sounds of the human voice as heard from a distance, that our senses are completely deceived. His art is not merely the clever producing of sounds, but the cultivation of such a fine degree of ear perception that he can distinguish the faintest differences in the tones reaching him, and is thus enabled to reproduce them. Many children have this gift, and so accurately perceive and register the sound impressions reaching them, that they are able to reproduce same with a considerable degree of skill.

Great differences are noticeable among individuals regarding the development of the sense of hearing. Some have a very keen ear for sounds in general, or sounds appertaining to certain lines of occupation, etc., but have but a very moderate, or even poor, degree of perception of musical tones, while on the other hand many musicians are notorious for their dullness of perception of outside sounds. Then again, some are able to distinguish certain kinds of sounds very readily, and scarcely notice others.

Our statement, in a previous chapter, that attention and interest is necessary before the mind will register a clear impression which can be readily reproduced, is particularly true in the case of impressions received through the sense of hearing. Good authorities have stated that "one-half of the deafness that exists, is the result of inattention." This being the case it will readily be seen that the best way to cultivate improved ear perception is to *cultivate attention and interest.* This, perhaps, will be more easily understood when we remember that in many cases we are almost perfectly oblivious to the sounds around us, being intently occupied with some other subject, in which case the sounds enter our ears freely, but the mind being otherwise occupied fails to take cognizance of the impressions received. In many instances, however, we will be able to remember things which were said which at the time we failed to hear. This is the effect of the subconscious function of the mind, of which we have spoken in another chapter.

It is a pity that in our modern life the training of the sense of hearing has been so much neglected. It is capable of affording us great pleasure and enjoyment as well as rendering us great service if educated and trained that we may receive from it the advantages which it is capable of affording. The sense of hearing may be more highly trained and developed than perhaps any of the other senses. It may be developed by exercise and culture and deteriorates by neglect and inattention. The Indian has such a wonderful sense of hearing, or rather has so trained his hearing, that he is enabled to hear the sound of the foot-steps of his approaching enemy by placing his ear to the ground. The mere rustling of a leaf or the cracking of a twig is distinctly heard by him. The leader of an orchestra will detect the faintest inharmony or departure from time or tune in his orchestra, and will be able to detect the faulty performer without hesitation. The blind being thrown back on their other senses, have developed these to a wonderful degree. They have so sharpened their sense of hearing, or rather the sense of attention and interest in sounds, that they can tell when they are passing a stationery object, by the sound of their own footsteps, and can discriminate between a lamp-post and a man standing still, by the same means.

We give below several exercises intended to develop the sense of hearing by practice. These exercises are intended principally as suggestions to the student, that he may be able to take advantage of the opportunities around him in his daily occupation calculated to develop this sense.

Exercise 1.

When passing along the street, endeavor to catch up and retain for a few moments the scraps of conversation of the passers-by overheard by you. You will be surprised at the number and variety of disconnected sentences you will be able to hear and retain in the course of a walk of a few blocks. It is all a matter of attention and interest. This exercise is, of course, valuable only in the way of practice, as the remarks overheard will probably be of no importance, unless you are a student of human nature.

Exercise 2.

Endeavor to distinguish between the voices of people you meet, and to remember the voice if you hear it again. Everyone has a different voice, and it is quite interesting to study the different types of voices and their characteristics. You will notice that every man has his own way of pronouncing and accenting certain words. You will also notice that persons from different countries, and from different parts of our own country, have different tones and peculiarities in speech. We have known traveling men who almost invariably could determine from what part of the country a person came, by merely hearing him speak. Then a person's character is often revealed by his voice, and the student of the subject will be able to form a very good idea of the speaker's mental make-up in this way. It may pay you to devote a little time and attention to this subject, in odd moments.

Exercise III.

An interesting exercise is that of standing where you cannot see the persons speaking, and endeavoring to distinguish their voices and to identify each speaker in turn. We have heard of a game of this sort, where a number of people sit behind a screen or curtain and speak a few words, endeavoring to disguise their voices. Those in front of the screen guess at the identity of the speaker. The result is said to be amusing, many finding it very difficult to recognize the voices of their best friends and relatives, while others who have paid more attention to voices will be able to identify the owner of every voice.

Exercise 4.

We knew a young woman employed in a large office building who could detect the slight difference in sound between the footsteps of every man having an office along the same long corridor. She claimed that each step had its own characteristics, and even went so far as to assert that the character of the walker revealed itself by the sound he made in placing his feet on the floor. There is a field here for one who wishes to study character at the same time developing his sense of hearing.

Exercise 5.

You will find it interesting and helpful to endeavor to remember the precise words that have been addressed to you during the course of the day just past. Very few people are able to correctly repeat that which has been said to them only a few moments before. Inattention is largely the cause. All employers know how little dependence can be placed in the attention and memory of the average employee in this respect. By cultivating your attention and memory along these lines, you may find it of advantage to you in your business life.

Exercise 6.

A useful exercise is that of listening to a simple piece of music, or a catchy tune, and then endeavoring to hum it over or whistle it. As simple as this may seem to be, it will prove to be a great help in ear training, and it will also develop the attention to sounds. Those who will practice it, will find that they are developing a new interest in tune, and will be able to enjoy music better than ever before.

Exercise 7.

You should attend all the lectures, sermons, addresses, etc., possible, and, paying strict attention to each, endeavor to afterwards jot down what you can remember of what you have heard. Review the address, and analyze it, and repeat as far as possible the words used. This is not only of value in developing ear perception and memory, but is one of the best possible means of becoming an expert speaker. Students who sit long under a favorite professor will gradually acquire more or less of his style, and the hearing of good speakers will gradually develop within the mind of the listener a power of expression far superior to that formerly possessed. This is particularly true if the student will endeavor to repeat sentences and expressions which he has heard. When one trains himself to memorize portions of the addresses of good speakers, and to repeat them as accurately as possible, not only the words but the tone and expression as well, he will find that he is developing within himself powers of delivery and expression which will prove quite useful in after life.

Exercise 8.

The best method of training the memory to retain and recall that which has been heard, is that used by the Hindus and other people in the transmission of their sacred teachings and philosophies, to which we have alluded in the preceding chapters. The keynote and secret of their wonderful system is *small beginnings; gradual increase; and frequent reviews.* In other chapters of this work, we will take up this system in detail, in connection with the practice of memorizing the contents of printed pages, etc., and we will merely go over it in general in this part of the book. The Hindu teachers begin by repeating a single line of their Vedas to the student. The latter memorizes this line thoroughly, imprinting both the words and their meaning upon his mind indelibly, so that he knows every word in the line as if it stood out before him. He can repeat the line backward or forward and knows the position of each word. Then he learns another line the next day, after which he reviews the first line, following it up with the second one just learned, thus joining then together in his mind. The next day a third line is added, the first two being reviewed and the third joined to them. And so on, one line each day, and constant review and joining together of the new line and the old ones. The *review* is, of course, the important thing, as it causes the student to go over and over the lines previously learned, each time the impression being deepened. These frequent repetitions also serve to rub smooth the line by which each line has been soldered to the succeeding and preceding ones, and makes the whole appear as if it had been learned at one time, thus giving a completeness to the composite impression. Later on, the student is able to take up two lines a day, then three and so on until an almost incredible capacity has been acquired. But the Hindu teachers warn against attempting too many lines a day for some time, as the mind must be gradually trained to the work.

To the student of this work, who desires to develop along these lines, we would advise that he have some friend help him in the work, reading a line to him the first day, and then repeating it until it is firmly fixed in his mind. Then the next day having him review the first line and learn the second, and then reviewing both. And so on, keeping to a single line a day for a month or so before attempting more. A line of poetry is the best thing upon which to commence. We do not know of a better poem for the purpose than Scott's "Lady of the Lake," the style of which is attractive, the rhythm pleasing, and the subject interesting. After hearing a line read the first time, the student should endeavor to repeat it. If he cannot repeat it clearly and plainly, he should have it re-read to him after a few minutes, and so on until he knows it thoroughly. He should then repeat it a number of times, until he thinks he knows it, and then he may try to say it backward. If he has so fixed it in his mind that he can make a mental picture of the words, he will have little difficulty after once acquiring the knack.

The second day he will repeat the line already learned, before he attempts the second line, and then, after learning the second line thoroughly in the way above stated, he should join the two together. On succeeding days he will add a line each day—one new line each day, remembering that the review is the thing that is the most important for him. He must think of the meaning of the words, as well as the mere words themselves, endeavoring to form a mental picture of what is being described. Do not attempt too much at the start. The one line a day will soon give you as much as you can well review without too much effort. Do not let the apparent simplicity and "easiness" of the task give you a poor idea of the plan. This is the same plan whereby the Hindu student or chela learns to commit to memory books equaling in size our Bible. Little by little, with constant reviewing, does he acquire this art.

We will take up this Hindu method at length in our chapter entitled the "Cumulative System," as before stated, in connection with the memorizing of printed words, but in this chapter on exercises in Ear Perception, we think it proper to call the attention of the student to the fact that if one wishes to remember what has been spoken in his presence, this is the one great way to do it. It is not merely the lines of the poem that you are learning, but you are also training and developing the ear and the mind to receive impressions, store them away, and then to recall them. You will find your aural memory increasing daily under this practice. It is worth all the trouble you bestow upon it.

In this exercise, if you find your interest fading, take up some new poem or subject, for a change, not forgetting to review the old lines from time to time. This change will give new zest to the exercise, and will enable you to go back to the old lines with renewed interest.

CHAPTER VIII.

ASSOCIATION.

Treating of that great law of the mind, upon which depends very much of the faculty of recalling, known as Association—The sequence of our thoughts is as much the result of a law as is the rising and falling of the tides. Our thoughts and recorded impressions are always associated in some way, although sometimes it is difficult to trace the connection—This chapter discusses the subject of Association, showing the several forms and the rules governing each. Next to Attention, this subject is the most important feature of Memory Culture, and the subject itself is full of interest and opens up a great field of thought.

Many of us fancy that our thoughts, when not impelled in a certain direction by the Will, come floating through our minds at random and in obedience to no law. When we see the apparent lack of connection between succeeding trains of thought we may be excused for holding such an opinion. But this idea is far removed from the real state of affairs, for although not clearly apparent, there is always a connecting link between one line of thought and the one succeeding it. The law of association governs here, and is just as inflexible as is the law of cause and effect in other fields—just as unvarying as is the law of gravitation. The sequence of our thoughts is as much the result of law as is the fall of the apple from the tree—the rise and fall of the tides. Our ideas are always associated in some way, although in many cases we cannot clearly trace the connection. They come in groups, and each group, in turn, is associated with some other group.

In a previous chapter we spoke of the important part in the subject of Memory Culture played by Attention. Next to Attention we find Association the most important feature of the subject. The recording faculty of the memory depends largely upon the degree of attention bestowed upon the object or subject to be remembered, while the reproducing function depends very materially upon the closeness of the association by which the impression is linked to other impressions which have been previously recorded. Authorities on psychology go so far as to claim that the law of association is to psychology what the law of gravitation is to physics. The habit of correct association is one of the most important requisites in the cultivation of the power of recollection.

In recording or storing away impressions, the best results are obtained when we concentrate our attention upon the thing under consideration. In recollecting these impressions, however, the best results are obtained by being able to associate the desired impression with one or more other impressions, the greater the number of associated impressions the greater the ease of recollection. Unless we have obtained a clear impression, the recalled impression will be imperfect, and, unless the impression be associated in some way with other impressions, we cannot recall it at all.

The principle of association is based upon that remarkable tendency of an impression to become so connected with one or more other impressions, that the recalling of one impression will bring into the field of consciousness the associated impressions. Bain says: "Associations that are individually too weak to operate a revival may succeed in so doing by acting together."

Ribot states that "the two principal facts which serve as a basis of association are resemblance and contiguity."

Association by resemblance depends upon the fact that an impression, either new or recalled, has a tendency to revive a previously recorded impression which resembles it in some particular, and the two thus become associated in the memory. The first impression may not have been previously associated with the second, and the latter may have been recalled only through a long chain of associations, but when the two have once been closely considered together, they are therefore associated closely and one may recall the other without making use of the heretofore necessary chain of association. The two impressions may have been originally recorded at times far apart from each other, and at different places, but when the resemblance is close, or is afterward made close by attention, they become as closely associated as if they were contiguous in time or place. The trained mind readily sees points of resemblance between apparently widely separated things, and this perceived resemblance records itself in the memory. Such a mind needs but to be given a start and it will bring into the field of consciousness an amazing chain of associated ideas, facts, incidents, illustrations, etc. On the other hand, the careless mind, having paid no attention to the relation between things, is unable to recall separated impressions by means of this principle of association by resemblance, and is able to recall only those things which are associated by contiguity.

Association by contiguity is like counting a string of beads of all kinds, one after the other, in the order in which they were strung, while association by resemblance is like pulling out a drawer in which has been placed everything we know concerning the matter under consideration, and taking therefrom article after article as it presents itself, chosing and selecting the best for the occasion, irrespective of the time in which they have been filed away. Impressions so associated are readily recalled when an occasion presents itself which calls for the aid of our past experiences and impressions, the occasion being the primary cause of the recall of all the information and accumulated experiences upon the subject that have been impressed upon our memory.

Association by contiguity depends upon the fact that an impression, either new or received, has a tendency to recall other impressions recorded at the same time, or in immediate succession. Impressions that are recorded in close succession have a tendency to so associate themselves and join themselves together, that the recollection of the one will usually recall the others. There is a strong affinity between an impression and the one which immediately precedes or follows it. It may be said that, generally speaking, there is no such thing as an isolated impression. Each impression is practically a continuation of a preceding one, and the beginning of a succeeding one. As Ribot says: "When we read or hear a sentence, for example, at the commencement of the fifth word something of the fourth word still remains. The end of the fourth word impinges on the beginning of the fifth."

In association by contiguity several impressions are recorded directly after the other, and when one is recalled it will bring the other in its train, and so on, from impression to impression. Thus it is easy to repeat a familiar sentence, word for word, as they occurred in the text, but we would find it quite difficult to repeat it backwards or to name haphazard the several words composing it. In a poem, the end of each word being associated with the beginning of the succeeding word, we find it easy to repeat them in that order, each word suggesting the next. The child repeats the alphabet, from A to Z, readily, but ask him to recite them from Z backwards to A and he will be unable to do it, unless he has practiced it in that order. Some persons who have acquired considerable proficiency in feats of memory are able to repeat hundreds of words by the aid of this form of association, but find themselves unable to commence at any particular part of their task if they are compelled to omit the part preceding it. We have heard the story of Leyden, who could repeat an entire Act of Parliament from beginning to end, without missing a word, but who was unable to take up any named portion of it without going over the preceding sections.

Many elaborate systems of mnemonics have been based upon this law of contiguous association, but while these systems, and many based upon the law of association by resemblance, have been found useful as an aid to memorizing, and are quite ingenious, they soon prove cumbersome and intricate and serve to confuse the memory rather than to develop it. Without attempting to follow these systems, however, the student will find it useful to cultivate this faculty of associating impressions, as it is much easier to recall impressions when they are closely associated with other impressions along the lines of contiguity. This faculty may be developed by exercises designed to concentrate the attention upon an impression and the one immediately succeeding it, or preceding it, so that the two may become practically welded together. Others may then be added until they are connected in such a way that to remember one is to recall all. The closer the contact the easier the recall—the sooner they are connected the more complete the welding. If the two impressions are not quickly and closely connected, there is always the chance that an irrelevant thought may come in between them and interfere with the contiguous association.

An understanding of this great law of association of impressions shows us that when we wish to store away an isolated fact in such a way that we may readily recall it, we must associate it with some other impression already stored away. The more we can associate a fact with other known facts, the more readily will we recall it, and the more associations we can give an impression the better it is for the purpose. Things which were originally contiguously associated, but which were associated by resemblance, may be made contiguously associated by their recall by resemblance several times in the same order, as they thus fall under the law of contiguity as well as the law of resemblance. The greater and more numerous the resemblances, the easier and surer the recall. The apparently wonderful powers of memory of miscellaneous facts possessed by some well-read and close-observing men, is due to the fact that they are able to find points of resemblance between widely separated facts, and are able to run from one set of facts to another in a way impossible to a man who has not cultivated the power of association by resemblance. Such men will practically take hold of a loose end of thought, and then simply unwind the ball.

CHAPTER IX.

REMEMBRANCE, RECOLLECTION AND RECOGNITION.

Treating of these three operations of the mind, which are frequently considered as being the same thing—The differences are pointed out and each term is clearly defined and explained—Remembrance is the word meaning that process of the memory whereby stored impressions come again into the field of consciousness, without an effort of the will, as by association, resemblance, etc.—Recollection is the word used to describe that process of the memory whereby a thing is recalled by an effort of the will—Recognition is that process of memory whereby, when we see or hear a thing, we know that we have seen or heard it before.

The three words forming the title of this chapter are frequently used as meaning practically the same thing. This is particularly true in the case of the first two mentioned words. But each of these words has a definite meaning, and refers to a distinct process of the memory.

Remembrance is the word meaning that process of the memory whereby previously stored impressions come again into the field of consciousness without an effort of the Will, as by association, resemblance, etc. Recollection is the word used to describe that process of the memory whereby a man recalls, by an effort of the Will, some impression previously stored away. Remembrance is apparently automatic in its action, while recollection is an act of volition, and is often accompanied with much effort. Recognition is the word applied to that process of the memory whereby, when we see or hear a thing, we know that we have seen or heard it before. It is a conscious association of the present impression with one had before. It is a re-cognizing—a re-knowing. If we see a thing on two different occasions, and do not "know" it when seen the second time, we do not recognize it, and the memory stores away two different impressions of the thing. If afterwards, we become aware of the identity of the two impressions, they become fused into one impression. Authorities lay down three laws of remembrance, as follows:

1. All impressions have a tendency to revive previous impressions of a similar character; but a previously received impression

will not thus be brought again into the field of consciousness, unless it be sufficiently distinct, unless the originally faint impression has been recalled to the consciousness by recollection and strengthened by repeated revivals.

2. An impression received similar to one previously received, if not recognized as being similar, will be stored away as a separate impression. But if the previous impression be recalled at the same time, and recognized as similar, the two impressions will be associated in the memory, and stored away together.

3. When a part of an associated series of impressions is revived, the other parts may be revived if desired with a minimum of effort; and the revival of an impression renders easier the revival of any impression received about the same time, without reference to resemblance.

In considering the first law of remembrance, we must not forget that one man may see a resemblance between things which appear to have no connection or resemblance to a second man. And this difference, of course, is carried out in the application of this law. If the resemblance is not seen or recognized, there is no association in the process of remembering.

The act of remembering is almost altogether a subconscious one and we are not consciously aware of its workings. We may be lost in thought and one subject after another passes before the consciousness, and we do not perceive the connection or association at the time. We can often, however, retrace the steps taken and can see the slight thread of connection between the different subjects of our thought. We may start by considering a table, and end by thinking of some totally different character of thing located at a far distant part of the world.

When we remember a thing it is generally because the association is natural, close and direct. When we are forced to recollect a thing we must use the Will to find connections and associations between a number of things before the missing impression is found. There is scarcely any conscious mentation required in the case of remembrance as compared with the process of recollection. The one is direct, and the other indirect.

We have spoken of the fact that it is most difficult to bring into the field of consciousness an impression but faintly recorded, while it is comparatively easy to so bring forth one that has been clearly and distinctly recorded by means of the attention. But a poor impression may be strengthened by a frequent revival, until it will become nearly or quite as distinct, and as easy to recall, as one of original clear recording. Impressions received under circumstances of great importance are apt to be clearly recorded, and consequently easily recalled.

We desire to call your attention to an important fact concerning the revival of impressions, and the consequent strengthening of the original impressions by the revival. It is the fact that the gist of the whole strengthening process lies in the conscious revival of the original impression, the holding of it before the field of consciousness by the attention, and the sending it back to the storehouse strengthened by the new amount of attention bestowed upon it. The conscious revival of a previous impression, and the new attention given it, is worth much more than the repeated viewing of the object originally causing the impression, at least so far as that particular impression is concerned. Of course a repeated view of the object will probably bring to light details which were not included in the first impression. We have spoken of this in our chapter on Eye Perception, and exercises.

In the same way, if, when you see a thing, a past impression is recalled and is thus associated, the old impression becomes a part of the new, and thereafter it is hard to separate them. We have much unavailable unused material in our memories, which might be of the greatest use to us if we had occasion to associate them. Sometimes we take up a new subject of thought, and form a connection and association between scores of disconnected facts which had been lying around loose in our mental storehouse.

Recollection is always accompanied with an effort of the will to find some chain of association which we desire to recall. This process may take but a fraction of a second, as the mind works very rapidly and the chain of association is soon formed. But often it takes some time before we are able to recall the desired thing, and many times we have to acknowledge our inability to bring forth the missing impression, but the orders given will often be taken up by the subconscious mentality and the impression will come into consciousness at some later time, often when we have ceased to think of the desire.

In recalling an impression one has often to recall the circumstances and place of the recording of the desired impression, or what took place just before or just after the fact he desires to recall. The mind instinctively calls upon the strongest faculty to supply the cue to the whole series of impressions.

In considering the matter of recognition, we see that there is that which may be called *full recognition,* and also another phase which may be termed *partial recognition.* When we meet a man whom we have previously met, and recognize his appearance, and remember his name, who he is, what he does, etc., we *fully* recognize him. But when we meet a man whose face we recognize, but whose name we fail to remember, or when we recognize his face, or even recognize his face and remember his name but fail to remember who he *is* and the circumstances of our former meeting, we have only *partially* recognized him. We remember hearing of a man who once met a lady whose face he recognized but whose name he could not remember. Falling back on the old expedient he said "Madam, I have forgotten the spelling of your name. Will you kindly tell me just how you spell it?" "Certainly," said the lady, "I spell it J-o-n-e-s." When we meet with a person who accosts us by name, and whose face we dimly recognize, but whom we "cannot place," we may remain in his company for a time, and then suddenly some allusion will give us the missing association and we remember clearly all that we have ever known about the individual.

There is a difference between remembering a thing and recognizing it. How many times have we sought for a thing which we distinctly *remembered* but which we were unable to find. Shortly after we found the thing in a place that we have looked over several times, and it is impossible that we did not *see* it. The trouble is that our faculty of recognition was not functioning properly, and although we saw the object we failed to recognize it. This trouble may be largely overcome by first forming a distinct mental image of the thing sought for, in which case we will recognize the object as soon as seen. This will apply to any object no matter how familiar we may be with it, as unless the mental image is sufficiently clear we will not recognize it even though we see it, our memory of it for the moment being merely a memory of name and not of appearance. A man may hunt for his wife in a crowd, and will not find her, although he may be looking her right in the face. His anxiety has driven away the mental image.

CHAPTER X.

GENERAL PRINCIPLES REGARDING IMPRESSIONS.

Treating of the thirteen general principles governing the subject of impressions—These thirteen principles practically sum up the entire subject of impressions, their acquirement, their retention, their recalling; and the knowledge of the same will enable the student to have the entire subject in a nutshell—Each principle is clearly stated, and is accompanied with explanations and illustrations—This chapter alone, if carefully studied, will give the student a liberal education in the theory and practice of Memory Culture, and might readily be expanded to fill a book.

The following principles will give a general idea of the laws governing the receiving, recording and revival of impressions received by the memory. The student will most likely find them interesting, and they may aid in fastening in his mind the laws governing the mental operations known to us as memory. Much that is said in this chapter is stated in other words in other parts of this book, but we have thought it advisable to bring these things together in one chapter, that the student might more readily associate one principle with another akin to it.

PRINCIPLE I. *Employ concentration so as to receive an impression sufficiently intense as to render easy a subsequent revival of the impression.*

As we have explained in previous chapters, it is necessary for the mind to be strongly directed toward the object or subject the impression of which we are desirous of recording in the mind in such a way as to be able to recall it with the least amount of exertion. Speaking generally, it may be said that the strength of the impression is in exact proportion to the amount of interest and attention bestowed upon the object or subject. Consequently it is of the utmost importance that we cultivate attention and interest, by practice, so as to be able to register a distinct impression. By doing this we have taken many steps toward the acquiring of a strong memory.

PRINCIPLE II. *Record definitely and decidedly the primary impression.*

Very much depends upon the sharpness of the primary impression. The primary impression is the foundation upon which subsequent impressions must be built, and if it be not distinct, it is very difficult to remedy the carelessness afterward, as in that case there has to be a tearing away of the primary impression, and a substitution of a new primary record, as otherwise there will be a confusion of memory. Therefore, in obtaining the first impression of an object or subject, direct upon it as much attention and interest as possible.

PRINCIPLE III. *At the beginning, avoid including too many details in the impression.*

This principle, if applied, will save the student much unnecessary work and waste of energy. The best plan is to master the main points of a subject at the beginning, then gradually build around these other important points. Then on to the less important, finishing up with the comparatively unimportant details. By forming a general idea of the subject to be studied, certain features will stand out more prominently. Study these first, getting a clear impression by omitting the lesser details, then stop and look over the subject again. You will then see other points standing out clearly. Take these up, and so on, until the subject is mastered. In this way you will be able to store away a complete record of the subject "from the ground up," and you will find it easy to recall to mind any part of it and at the same time be aware of the relation of that part to any other part. This is the only rational plan of study. It will help you in following this method, to think of the subject to be mastered as being a tree. Commence at the ground and thoroughly understand the trunk, then take up the larger limbs, then the branches, then the twigs. In commencing the study of a new subject, it is better to read first the most elementary work on the subject to be found, and after mastering this take up a work rather more advanced, and so on. Many make the mistake of reading at first the most complete work on the subject to be had, and the consequence usually is that they master no point completely, and have merely a vague idea of the entire subject. Some teachers advise the careful study of the subject as stated in some standard encyclopædia. before even taking up the elementary text book. The rule of Nature is that we shall "crawl before we walk," and study and memorizing is no exception to the rule.

PRINCIPLE IV. *By reviving an impression frequently, you increase its intensity.*

The whole subject of Memory Training depends so much upon this one principle, that if we were compelled to take away this principle the whole structure would fall. Remember now, we are speaking of the conscious revival of the original impression, and not of the receiving of a subsequent impression. By this method, not only is the impression intensified, but the Will is trained to assist, and in a short time the recalling of the impression becomes almost automatic. By constant review, a subject becomes almost indelibly impressed upon the mind, and is recalled with the least possible effort. If you have observed the first three rules, you will have received impressions with a considerable degree of clearness, and by regular practice and reviewing you will be able to obtain a wonderfully deep and permanent impression of the subject under consideration. A leading writer on this subject, illustrates this principle by the case of a man meeting a stranger and spending a whole evening in his company, but yet being unable to recognize him when he sees him a few days later. The writer points out that if the stranger had been seen for only five minutes a day for a fortnight, he would have been easily recognized, the constant repetition of the impression recording it strongly in his mind.

PRINCIPLE V. *When reviving an impression, do it so far as possible without referring to the object itself, thus obtaining the greatest permanent intensity.*

We have touched upon this principle in the chapter on Eye Perception. The idea is that the impression should be revived mentally so far as is possible. Of course, it will be found that details have not been noticed, and it will be necessary to go back to the object to supply the things omitted, but first endeavor to recall plainly that which *has* been noticed, and thus intensify the impression. The details subsequently acquired are to be treated in the same way, each revival of impression including more details and being more complete. If you were to simply go and look at an object in a general way every day for a month you would not know half as much about it as would be the case if you had studied it carefully the first time, and then tried to mentally reproduce it either in the imagination or on paper by aid of a pencil, and then repeated the process every day for a week, acquiring fresh details each day. In the latter case the second day's inspection would only include the points that had not been intensely impressed by the first day's view, and the new points closely observed would be added to the first day's impressions when both were reviewed or revived. "An unheard lesson is soon forgotten."

PRINICIPLE VI. *When practicing, revive the previous impression of the subject or object, rather than attempt to receive a new impression.*

This principle closely resembles the preceding one, and teaches that we should rely upon our memory as much as possible, instead of flying back to the subject or object as a whole, as soon as we find that we cannot easily recall any detail. *Use* the memory and thus strengthen it, instead of using it only when made necessary by the absence of the object itself. To do otherwise would be like keeping a copy of the multiplication tables handy to refer to whenever we had to multiply two figures, because that would be easier than taking the trouble to exercise our memory. If we depend upon the receiving of a new impression instead of the revival of the old one, we will never really learn anything, and will be constantly compelled to go back to learn our lesson over again.

PRINCIPLE VII. *When a subject or an object is being studied for the first time, and therefore no previous impression has been recorded, it is well to think of a similar impression so as to establish a mental association.*

This principle renders somewhat easier the receiving of impressions of a new object, as by connecting the new thing with something already learned, you gain the advantage of the association and the benefit of attaching the new impression to one that is already well fixed in the mind. It is akin to the observing of a new detail of an object and the including of that new detail in the next review, thus gaining the advantage of the previous strong impression and having a peg upon which to hang the new impression. If you meet a man named Thompson, and find it hard to recall the name, you will find it a material help to think of that man as having the same name as another friend of yours whose name is also Thompson, and whose name you never forget. The two men and their names are thus linked together in your memory, and you will find it very easy to remember the new acquaintance's name after forming the association. And in the study of a new subject, endeavor to connect it with the subject nearest associated to it, which you already know. If you can connect a thing with something similar to it, the mind will make the new thing a part of the old, and will not treat it as a newcomer. The mind seems to be somewhat conservative, and to get along better with a new acquaintance if it thinks it is related to an old friend.

PRINCIPLE VIII. *It is well to establish a series of mental associations, so that one impression may revive the next of the series and so on.*

When one part of a thing is remembered, the mind very readily recalls other parts of the same thing, and so when we join a number of things together, thus forming a chain, each link being a part of the whole, we will find it comparatively easy to start at any link and run backward or forward over the entire length of the chain. It is well to form the different parts of a subject into sort of a series, arranging the parts in logical order so far as is possible. A new part may afterwards be inserted in its proper place, and recalled just as well as the old portions. The effect of association in recalling objects or subjects is wonderful. It is very much easier for a child to remember the letter H because he knows G, and associates H with it. And we will find that our memory of many subjects is strikingly like that of the child's memory of the alphabet or multiplication table, so far as association is concerned. If you cannot remember a thing just when you desire to do so, the next best thing is to have a loose end which you can unwind until you get the desired thing. It would bother the average man to call off at random the names of the cross streets in the center of his city, but if he will start at the first one he will be able to run them off in proper order without much trouble. In the same way it is easy for the school-boy to name the Presidents of the United States, or the Kings of England, commencing with Washington or William the Conqueror, as the case may be. But ask him to "mix them up" and give you the entire list and he will find it a very difficult task. We will find that the things we remember best are connected in our mind with something that came before or just after, or which in some other way bear some orderly relation to the remembered thing. In forming the mental series, follow the rule of the alphabet, or list of Presidents, and fasten the first one in your mind firmly, then add on the next, etc.

PRINCIPLE IX. *In the study or investigation of a subject or an object, use as many faculties as possible.*

The value of this principle is perceived when we remember that each faculty registers upon the mind a separate impression, and when we use more than one faculty in the study of a thing, we receive as many sets of impressions as we have used faculties. If we are trying to commit a name or a date to memory, it will aid us materially if, in addition to repeating the name or date, we will write it down and study it with the eye, thus receiving the abstract impression of the thing, its sound, and the visual impression. In recalling it we may be helped either by the general remembrance of it, by its sound, or by our recollection of how it looked when written on paper. Many persons giving public recitations say that the position of certain words and paragraphs appear before their mind's eye, just as they were on the page of the book from which the lines were read. Preachers who prepare their sermons in manuscript and study them over at home, going to the pulpit with only general notes or with no notes at all, tell us that they will see the position of each paragraph, and the first word of same, just before they reach it, looking just at it did in their manuscript. Public speakers experience the same thing.

Many persons find themselves unable to remember a name unless they repeat it aloud once or twice. Many instances of the application of this principle will occur to you as you progress in your work of training the memory.

PRINCIPLE X. *You may greatly improve weak faculties by exercises adapted to each.*

When you find it difficult to recall impressions previously received from any particular faculty, it is well to begin training and developing that faculty to the end that it may register sharper impressions. Other chapters of this book will suggest many methods and ways of doing this. By developing a number of faculties, you will receive a greater number of intense impressions, and will, consequently, find it much easier to recall the thing wanted, as a greater number of impressions have been made sharply, and can be more easily found when wanted.

PRINCIPLE XI. *Difficulty in recalling an impression may be overcome by endeavoring to revive an impression received at the same time, or by trying to recall some associated component.*

An instance of the application of this principle, is had in the case of one who fails to recall a name. Try as he will the name will not come into the field of consciousness. He then begins to run over the alphabet, slowly, pausing at each letter and considering it before passing on. Very often the thought of the first letter of the name will bring back the impression of the name itself. The initial letter of a name is often remembered more clearly than the balance of the name, and the latter is brought by association when the mind recalls the first letter. If this method fails, try the plan of trying to remember the person himself, how he looked and talked, when and where you first heard his name, etc., or if it be the name of a thing, apply the same rule, and try to recall the circumstances surrounding it, the qualities connected with the thing bearing the name, etc.

PRINCIPLE XII. *In endeavoring to recall an impression, think of some definite thing connected with it and revive others received about the same time. This is better than trying to recall it in an indiscriminate way.*

When you are unable to succeed by the application of Principle XI, and can recall no impression received at the same time or component part, endeavor to recall the impression of something connected with the thing, in some way, getting as close to the object or subject as possible, and, if possible, the circumstances connected with the obtaining of the impression. Imagine yourself back in the position and under the circumstances that existed when the impression was received, and often you will start into operation a train of thought which will bring the desired thing into the field of consciousness.

PRINCIPLE XIII. *When a previous impression is recalled, involuntarily, by the mind, after a previous unsuccessful attempt to recall it voluntarily, it is well to note the associated reviving impression, for future use and experiment.*

This involuntary recollection of a thing which the mind has previously refused to recall, is, of course, an effort of the subconscious function of the mind. But, a little careful investigation will show that it came into the field of consciousness following closely another thought, although the connection between the two may not be apparent at first sight. By remembering the reviving impression, that is the impression which came into the field of consciousness just before the elusive impression, you may bring back the troublesome thing at will, no matter how long afterward the time may be when the word is again forgotten. And the noting of the dim connection will often open up quite a field for thought and give the key to a further knowledge of the great subject of memory.

CHAPTER XI.

THE CUMULATIVE SYSTEM OF MEMORY CULTURE.

Treating of a rational, practical, easily acquired system of Memory Culture, which in the opinion of the author of this book is the best and only practical method of developing the Memory as a whole—This is a modern presentation of the system used by the ancients, in India, Greece, Iceland, and other countries, to train the minds of students that they might acquire and store away the legends, religious books, philosophies, and laws of the races, and by means of which it was a common thing for these pupils to memorize books exceeding in size our Bible—Full instructions and directions are given for the development of the memory by this great system.

Those who have made a careful study of the subject of Memory Culture, and who have no pet hobbies to ride or fads to promote, generally agree that the method which we term "The Cumulative System" is the only natural system of developing the power of memory. It depends upon no set of tricks, catch-words, etc., but proceeds on the theory that the development of memory must be gradual, and by easy stages. It seeks to *develop* the memory, instead of loading it down with "methods." Its underlying theory is the memory may be developed just as one would develop a muscle or part of the body—gradually, and by easy exercises constantly repeated. It is not a trick method of committing things to memory, but a system of developing and training the memory until it can readily recall things without the necessity of any tricks or artificial methods. It is Nature's own way of doing things—of developing from the seed to the plant. But at the same time it affords the best possible plan of committing to memory anything of great length.

This "Cumulative System" is not a new system. It is merely the oldest system revived. It is the system used by thê Orientals and other ancient people in training the mind to carry without mistake their sacred teaching and philosophies. In other parts of this work we have given numerous examples of the wonderful feats of memory performed by these peoples, and from what we have seen in a number of modern cases there seems to be no reason for thinking that these same feats may not be duplicated by the people of to-day. There is a very good reason for the apparent discontinuance of the old system. In the old days before printing was discovered, but very few people could write, and the writings themselves were apt to be mislaid, lost or destroyed, and the teachers were afraid to trust their teachings to parchment or whatever material happened to be in use. So they would train the minds of their pupils until they could commit to memory works of the same size as our Bible, or even larger. As you will see by reference to other chapters, the philosophies, religious books, and even the laws of many nations were thus transmitted and perpetuated for many centuries, without being committed to writing at all. Even in our own days, the rituals of secret societies are transmitted in this way, the rules of the orders prohibiting the writing or printing of certain parts of their ritual, or in some cases of any of it.

With the dawn of printing, when it became apparent that when thousands of copies of a book might be printed, and the chance of loss reduced, the necessity for the oral transmission of the teachings passed away, and the old art of memorizing almost entirely passed away. Men found it not worth while to memorize things which they could find in the books on their shelves. They overlooked the fact that in allowing the old system to pass out of use, they not only lost the art of memorizing matters of great length, but they also lost the art of training the memory to remember ordinary things, and the result is seen in our condition to-day, when a man of good memory is looked upon as a curiosity. Moreover, many have grown to believe that a good memory is almost an abnormal thing and that the natural condition of man is to have a poor memory. They do not realize that every man has the power to develop his memory very far beyond its present condition. Of course, some men naturally remember better than others, but the man with a poor memory may so develop it by proper training that he can remember better than can the man with a good memory without training.

The "Cumulative System" differs from other systems, inasmuch as it does not teach how to remember a thing by its association with another thing which is perhaps more easily remembered, or with some thing already fixed in the memory. Instead of this it endeavors to so develop, strengthen and train the mind that it is enabled to easily commit to memory anything which it desires, and is also able to easily recall the thing memorized, by Will.

One of the beauties of this system is that while you are practicing you are committing to memory valuable information and knowledge, and while you are committing interesting and useful things to memory, you are developing the memory itself. It must be remembered, however, by the student that the great importance of the system lies not in the mere ability to memorize long poems, speeches, etc., but in the developing and strengthening of the memory itself. And not only does it develop in one the power of storing away impressions in the mind, but also trains one in the faculty of recollection—in recalling readily that which has been memorized. The result of an earnest study and application of this system is that (1) the special thing studied will be easily memorized, long remembered and readily recalled; (2) there will be a marked and steady increase in the power of memorizing *anything;* and (3) a marked increase and growth of the power of recalling *anything* by an effort of the Will.

The "Cumulative System" is based upon the theory that the power of memorizing and recollection may be enormously increased by a system of progressive exercises and *by frequent reviews.*

The student should select something to commit to memory that interests him, and the subject of which is pleasant. A favorit poem, if long enough, is good. We think that Scott's "Lady of the Lake" is one of the best poems for this purpose, although the student may select any other if he prefers it. The Book of Proverbs, or the Psalms are also good, and some minds find it easier to memorize verses from the Bible than poetry.

Commence by committing to memory one verse from the Bible, or one verse of a poem, providing the verses of the latter contain not more than four or six lines. If longer, it will be better to divide up the verse into sections of not over the number of lines named. Learn this verse well, until you can repeat it readily, and understand it in all its parts. Learn not only its sound when read aloud, but also its looks in print; its leading words; the arrangement; its meaning. In short, *learn* it. This will be enough for the first day.

On the second day the verse of yesterday should be reviewed and repeated aloud. Then another verse should be learned in the same way, and then joined to the first verse and the two reviewed.

On the third day the two verses previously learned should be reviewed, and a third verse thoroughly learned, and then joined to the previous verses, and then reviewed as a whole.

Continue this exercise for a month, learning and adding one verse each day, and reviewing as a whole frequently. We cannot impress upon you too often the necessity of frequent reviewing. The gist of the whole matter is in the reviewing, so do not shirk this part of the work in the slightest. The continual addition of verses memorized tends to develop the faculty of *memorizing,* whereas the constant reviewing is for the purpose of developing and strengthening you in the direction of easy *recollection.* It is not sufficient merely to obtain good clear mental impressions, but it is of vital importance for you to be able to locate and bring out the things stored away in your mental storehouse. You not only get acquainted with the particular articles you are bringing out every day, but are also developing the "knack" of finding things in the mental storehouse, and of bringing them to view when wanted.

At the beginning you will probably find that it is often necessary to refer to the book to supply a missing word or line. Do not let this discourage you, for you will soon overcome it. And do not unduly strain the memory by a forced effort to recall the elusive word or line, but take up the book and learn that particular verse over again. If necessary refer to the book a dozen times rather than to go on omitting words or being in a state of uncertainty about their correctness. Do not go on in a slipshod manner, but insist upon exactness and absolute correctness. By insisting upon this from the start, the mind will soon take on that quality.

Do not miss a day's exercise. You will find it far better to learn a few lines each and every day than a greater number every few days. The will and the memory are both strengthened by regular exercise and practice. The entire series of exercise will be found to strengthen and develop the will power of the student, and the strength thus gained will be found most useful in other fields of work.

At the beginning of the second month, learn *two* verses a day instead of one verse. Keep this up during the second month, learning two verses each day, and reviewing the verse previously memorized, both those of the first month and the verses learned after the two-verse plan has been adopted. You will find that the second month's work is no more difficult than that of the first month. The two-verse task will be as easy as the one-verse exercise. You will find that your memory has anticipated the increase. and that you can easily learn three or even four verses each day, but stick to the two verses, and do not attempt to get ahead of your lesson. The efficacy of this system lies largely in the fact that it leads the student *gradually,* and develops him in Nature's own way. And, remember that in the *reviewing* lies the secret of increased powers of recollection.

At the beginning of the third month, commence with *three* verses, and proceed as before, adding each day to your store, and reviewing each day that which you have previously learned. When the fourth month comes adopt the four-verse plan, and so on. Of course there is a limit to this constant increase, of which we will speak a little later on. This limit will be found to vary with the individual, but the most backward student will be able to attain wonderful proficiency with very little effort, by following the gradual and progressive method.

If the reviewing after a few months takes up more time than you have to spare, drop the new verses and devote the entire time to reviewing. And later on if you cannot review the whole thing in the time at your disposal in one day, divide it in two, and review the first half to-day and the rest to-morrow.

If, after a time, the task of committing additional verses to memory, seems tiresome, it will be as well to discontinue this part of the work for a short time, but keep up the reviewing, devoting all the time usually devoted to the exercise to the review work alone. Sometimes that part of the mind which attends to the work of receiving impressions will rebel at its daily task, but the other part of the mind which we use to recall things already impressed there will prove to be bright and perfectly willing to work.

The student will find that certain ways of doing this work best suited to his particular temperament, etc., will suggest themselves to him. He may vary and improve on the plan we have given here, providing always that he does not slight the review work, which must not be omitted or cut down. Cut down the memorizing if you must, but hold fast to the review work. The increased strength of the memory lies in the work of frequent reviews. This review work, although somewhat tedious at first, will soon grow to be a pleasant occupation, and then the pleasure of the conscious increase in mental power will render the task most interesting.

If you have not the time to devote to the full carrying out of this system, as herein laid down, you may vary it by learning short poems by this method, and after thoroughly mastering one, so that it may easily be reviewed at any time, pass on to another, devoting all your time and attention to the new one when learned. But when the second one is learned, go back to the first one and review it. Continue reviewing the ones you have learned, at odd times, or occasionally, and devote your daily review work to the one on hand until it too is thoroughly learned. Exercise the faculty of recollection by frequently recalling things which you have learned in the past, as each time you give yourself this exercise you strengthen the faculty.

If you lose interest in the particular thing you are memorizing, lay it aside for a while, and take something of a different character by way of a change, not forgetting to occasionally review the one laid aside.

You will probably find that some verses of a poem are more easily remembered than others. But do not slight the difficult ones, in fact you should bestow upon them more time and attention than upon the favorite ones. There is some reason for the trouble with the difficult verses, and by keeping at the work until you conquer, you will be strengthening some weak spot in the faculty of memorizing or recollection, and will be gaining additional will-power besides.

After you have been practicing this system for a number of months, you will find that you will be able to retain any particular thing in your memory with less frequent reviews, and you may vary your plan to accommodate yourself to your increased powers, and review well learned subjects only once in a while. But it is well to review a little of *something* every day in order to give the faculty something upon which to work.

You will also come to a point, sometime, where you will realize that you have reached your limit in the matter of the number of lines or verses to be memorized at any one time. You cannot go on forever increasing your limit at the rate of one additional daily verse each month. When this time is reached, stop the monthly increase, and rest on your oars so far as the increase of the daily work is concerned. Keep on with the work of memorizing and reviewing, but limit your lines or verses to the highest easily memorized number. Remember that the main purpose of the exercises is not to see how much you can do, but simply to give you training and development. After stopping for a time, without any attempt to increase, you may find, all of a sudden, that you are able to master a much heavier daily memory task. But whether you do or do not, matters little. And in any event you will find that your power of *recollecting* steadily increases, apparently having no limit.

Learn a thing thoroughly before going to the next. It is better to know one thing thoroughly, than ten things partially. Do not pass on to another verse until you have mastered the one upon which you have been working.

Do not attempt to "rush" matters. Take your time. And do not attempt too much at first. The average student is too eager. He starts off with a rush, and is apt to tire before he has gone very far. Better hold yourself in a little, and develop naturally as does the plant which grows from seed to shoot; from shoot to stalk; from stalk to leaves; from leaves to flower.

Do not attempt to do this work when you are tired or worn out. In such condition you will fail to receive clear impressions or to recall clearly and distinctly. Many find the morning the best time in which to practice.

CHAPTER XII.

THE TEN-QUESTION THOUGHT SYSTEM.

Treating of a novel and rational method of bringing forth from the subconscious store-house the miscellaneous assortment of information which every person has stored away regarding various subjects, but which knowledge is unavailable and unused because of the lack of system in the storing away, and the absence of knowledge of a method whereby this scattered knowledge may be brought together—This system, if mastered and practiced, will immensely increase the available information at the disposal of one, and will render one "well informed" upon subjects of which he apparently knows but little—It is an eye opener, and will produce remarkable results—This chapter also contains an explanation of "Analytical Memorizing."

Every man has in his subconscious storehouse a vast assortment of general information or knowledge. He knows something about every object or subject which has ever attracted his attention or interest in the faintest degree. The character and amount of such knowledge of course depends largely upon the degree of attention he has bestowed upon it, and upon the opportunities for observation he may have had in the past. But even the man of the most limited opportunities and the most careless observation has stored away much valuable material of whose existence he is almost unaware. The information has been stored away mechanically, and no attempt to resurrect it has been made, as no demand for the stored away knowledge has been apparent in the man's every day life.

If we would by intelligent practice occasionally bring forth to the light of day the stored away knowledge we would give our minds beneficial practice; increase our powers of recollection, broaden our field of available knowledge; develop our powers of reasoning, comparison, etc., and make ourselves "better informed" regarding a variety of subjects. The bringing forth of these stored-up memories will compel us to classify them, arrange them in their proper order, make comparisons, note associations, draw conclusions, and make use of a variety of our mental faculties, which will result in mental development and culture. Many of us are like misers who have hoarded away precious metal, which we never again see or make use of.

The writer has heard of prisoners, and men compelled to live away from congenial companions, compelled to look to themselves for company, who turned their vision inward and evolved from their inner consciousness the knowledge which had been stored there, and directed their mental processes to the same, with the result that when they emerged from their seclusion they had attained a degree of mental development far in advance of that possessed by them when they entered it. There are cases of record where political prisoners have written the most interesting books during their confinement, without having a single reference book, their information being drawn from that great storehouse, the subconscious mentality. Men sometimes live in a community taking casual notes regarding the people and things around them, with no special object in view. Years afterward, these men find themselves writers, and draw upon their old, almost forgotten, impressions of the past, and putting them on paper give to the world a vivid picture of the life of the town or city of their former abode. Dumas has given us an example of this subsequent use of stored-up knowledge in his well known novel "The Count of Monte Cristo." He shows us the old political prisoner, the Abbe Faria, who has been shut out from the sight of men for years, resurrecting his old fund of information for the benefit and instruction of his fellow prisoner, Edmond Dantes, and exciting the interest and concentrated attention of the latter he develops him from a bright but uneducated fisherman-sailor into a well-informed and educated man of the world. The old Abbe has stored away in his mind the learning of a lifetime, and draws from it for the benefit of Dantes. The story is, of course, pure fiction, but given the circumstances and the men, there is no reason why the result could not be obtained.

This resurrecting of stored-away impressions has another good result. It awakens in one an interest in the subject or object under consideration, and the mind thereafter will be awake to impressions concerning the object or subject, and one's fund of information regarding that particular thing, and things associated with it, will be greatly augmented. The mere directing of the attention upon the subject or object, after placing oneself where he will not be distracted by outside impressions, or after shutting out impressions if he has the power, will bring into the field of consciousness many interesting impressions and important information. But if one pursues a systematic plan for bringing out the impressions, his power of recollection will be greatly increased, and at the same time his mind will be developed along the lines of systematic thinking, classification, analysis, etc.

The writer has found the following system of "resurrecting thought" quite useful in his own case, and in that of others to whom he has presented the matter. It is simple but wonderfully effective, and its continued use will undoubtedly repay one for the time and trouble expended upon it. It increases brain-power, in several directions, and is a most effective educational method.

The system consists of ten questions, which when applied to the object or subject under consideration, and answered by bringing into the field of consciousness all the stored-up impressions to be found there, will be found to have brought into play all the information concerning that particular thing possessed by the student. The following outline will give an idea of the system. The subject is to be first stated, and then the nine questions asked of oneself and answered, one by one.

QUESTIONS REGARDING THE SUBJECT OR OBJECT.

I. Its origin or root?
II. The reason of its inception?
III. Its history?
IV. Its qualities and characteristics?
V. Things associated with and connected with it?
VI. Its use and application?
VII. It demonstrates what?
VIII. Its results and consequences?
IX. Its end or future?
X. Your general opinion regarding it, and your reasons for same.

You will find that this system of questions will bring to light all of your previous impressions regarding the thing under consideration, and also will cause you to classify, arrange, consider, pass upon and determine its various features. It will educate you in recollecting, thinking, studying and observing. Each question will suggest something to you, and when you are through with the subject you will find that you know much more about it than you thought possible. Besides this, you will commit the questions to memory, and your observation and study of anything thereafter will naturally be along the lines of the questions.

Do not let the apparent simplicity of this system cause you to pass it by without trial. Give it at least one trial on a subject, under favorable circumstances, and you will begin to see its uses. Of course, the ability to recall impressions, in answer to the questions, will steadily increase with practice, after the mind becomes accustomed to the inquisitorial process. Try the system on a subject this week, and then repeat the process a week later, and you will find a great improvement, your fund of impressions regarding that subject having apparently grown materially during the interval. The explanation is that your questions have started to work the sub-conscious searchers who have been at work digging out treasures from the depths of the great storehouse. Your questions have been regarded as orders from the Will, and these little workers have been busy with their imposed task, while your consciousness was busy with other things.

ANALYTICAL MEMORIZING.

When one wishes to master a subject, it will be found advisable that he dissect that subject—analyze it thoroughly, and by thus examining its parts in detail obtain a comprehensive idea of it as a whole. This mental dissection will arouse the faculties to activity, and will cause the memory to receive intense impressions which will be readily recalled.

It has been found that by a little analytical work the *meaning* of a thing is brought out so plainly that the mind will readily grasp it and hold on to it. The best way to investigate a thing is to ask questions about it. The best way to bring out your knowledge of a subject is to ask yourself questions about it, as we have shown in the first part of this chapter. The best way to fix a thing in your mind is to ask yourself questions calculated to bring out its full meaning.

To illustrate this idea, let us take the well known line:

"The curfew tolls the knell of parting day,"

and dissect or analyze it. What does the curfew *do?* It *tolls* the knell of parting day. *What* tolls the knell of parting day? The *curfew.* *What* does the curfew toll? It tolls the *knell.* The knell of *what* does it toll? The knell of *parting day.* The knell of what part of the day does the curfew toll? The knell of *parting* day. The knell of parting *what?* The knell of parting *day.* If you have gone over the above questions and answers, in earnest, you will never forget this line. It will stand out clearly in your mind.

In the above sentence the *active* word is, of course, the *verb,* tolls, and the rest of the sentence is dependent upon its active part. The attention, as a rule, is attracted by a moving thing more readily than by something at rest, and if the *action* of the verb is impressed on the mind, the rest of the sentence will be connected with it by the law of association. It helps the memory to *picture* the verb's meaning in the mind. In committing a thing to memory, find out what it all *means,* by this analytical method, and you will have simplified matters very materially.

CHAPTER XIII.

MEMORY OF FIGURES, DATES AND PRICES.

Treating of the development of the memory upon these most interesting lines, which are so important to the man and woman in their every-day and business life—There is nothing so annoying to the student as to forget dates, and the failure to remember prices and figures has proved the undoing of many a promising young business man—This chapter goes into the subject clearly, and gives explanations of poor memory along these lines, and points out the methods whereby improvement may be had—Exercises and directions are given, which will prove valuable to the student.

There is a great difference between persons regarding the remembrance of dates, prices, figures, etc., the difference being caused by the varying degrees of development of the faculty of number. Those in whom this faculty is largely developed will invariably store away a clear and lasting impression of figures and everything connected with them, while those in whom the faculty is deficient will find it quite difficult to remember anything connected with the subject. The latter class should develop the faculty by making use of it in the direction of having much to do with figures, especially in the branch of mental arithmetic. If you are one of this class, buy an elementary Mental Arithmetic, such as is used in the primary grades of schools, and carefully study it, working out every example given. Take up one lesson every day, and in a short time you will find that you are developing quite an interest in figures, and are beginning to remember them much better. The most satisfactory results may be obtained from practice of this kind. The development thus gained is permanent, and the faculty will continue to develop and register clearer impressions of figures and all concerning them.

DATES.

To those who find difficulty in remembering or recalling dates, the plan of forming a mental image of the date as attached to some important character or thing connected with the date has proven helpful. For instance, suppose that you wish to remember the year of the discovery of America by Columbus. You will find it easy if you will form a mental picture of Columbus standing on the shores of the newly-discovered land, with the figures 1492 over his head. Or if you wish to remember the date of the Declaration of Independence, form the picture of Liberty Bell with 1776 painted on it in bright figures. Or, in the case of the beginning of the Civil War, the mental picture of Fort Sumter with 1861 appearing on its sides in large figures. Or the date of Napoleon's death, by the mental picture of his tomb with 1821 graven on its side. In forming the mental picture it is well to have the date marked on a piece of paper, in large figures, upon which the eye should intently gaze while the mental picture is built around the figures. Then close the eyes, or turn away the head, and revive the impression. If this is done several times the memory of the figures will be indelibly impressed upon the mind.

We know of a schoolboy who remembered the beginning and ending of the term of each President by marking the dates upon the foreheads of each, in the pictures of his school history, but we scarcely advocate the following of this plan. A strong mental image may be formed by the average person, and when a strong impression of the date, accompanying the person or object, is stored away, it is likely to prove permanent and the associated impressions will always appear when the subject is recalled.

The above plan proves of the greatest value to those whose "eye memory" is good. In some cases, however, the "ear memory" is better, and in such cases it will be found that the verbal repetition of the date by the student, or better still by a friend, will fix the sound in the memory so that it may be readily recalled. Others find that they can best remember dates by doggerel rhymes committed to memory, such as—

"In fourteen hundred and ninety-two
Columbus sailed the ocean blue."

"In eighteen hundred and sixty-one
America's Civil War begun."

"In seventeen hundred and seventy-six
Jonathan taught John Bull a few tricks."

"In eighteen hundred and twenty-one,
At last did set Napoleon's sun."

"In eighteen hundred and ninety-eight
The Spanish fleets did meet their fate.

For in that year, the first of May,
Dewey entered Manila Bay;
And two months later, on third of July,
Cervera's fleet was sunk by Schley."

The average schoolboy has no trouble in composing this grade of doggerel to order, and many an important date and event has been memorized in this way.

But of all the above plans of memorizing dates, we prefer the first mentioned plan of "visualizing," or forming a mental image of the date in connection with the person or object connected with the date. It is more easily acquired than might be imagined, and after a little practice becomes almost automatic. One can form a mental picture of almost any historical event, and the portraits of the leading characters in history may readily be recalled.

In the case of students who have many important dates to remember, it is a good plan to connect the name of the person or event with the date, by the law of associated impressions. By always speaking of "Waterloo 1815"; or "Yorktown 1781"; or "Hastings 1066," the dates of these battles will become inseparably associated with the events themselves, and the two impressions will become fused. Of course, this will require the frequent repetition of the event and associated date, to fix the combined impression in the mind. If the date and event had been associated in this way from the beginning, there would have been no more trouble about the association than in the case of the words "Washington" and "George," or "Napoleon" and "Bonaparte." If we had not heard Washington's first name, or Napoleon's last name, until long after we had formed a clear impression of the other name of each, we would have sometimes forgotten the last learned name, whereas, having learned them both together, the two names are practically one so far as our memory is concerned. If teachers would always speak of "Waterloo 1815," the students would never forget the date of that battle, so long as they remembered its name.

PRICES.

The above mentioned plan of forming a mental image associating the figures with the object is of the greatest importance to clerks, salesmen, etc., whose work requires them to remember the price of goods. In many cases the clerk may actually *see* the prices attached to the goods by reviving the impression several times when looking at the goods in question. We know of a young man who was employed in a large retail grocery store who would form a mental image of this kind of every new lot of goods placed on the shelves, and who always thought of the goods as being plainly marked. If anyone asked him the price of "Baker's Chocolate," he would think of the package with the price marked upon it, and he knew the price of hundreds of articles of every description without referring to them except mentally. When the price changed he would wipe out the old mental figure and replace it with the new price. Today, after the lapse of over twenty years, he is able, by a mental effort, to recall the picture and price of the majority of the goods carried in the old store, the impression coming as a mental picture of the article with the price attached. His faculty of locality is large, and he is able to mentally rebuild the old store shelves, bearing upon them the goods just as they appeared twenty years ago, prices and all. If you will clearly associate the price with the appearance of the goods, the mental picture of the latter will bring with it the recollection of the former, and perhaps even the figures themselves will appear in the "mind's eye."

FIGURES.

Figures other than dates or prices may be associated with any object to which they would naturally be attached. But if there is no such appropriate object to which to attach the figure, the simple "visualizing" method must suffice. This method consists in photographing the figures upon the mind, until the mind will recall the details and shape of the figures, as it will those of a picture. Imagine the figures painted in large white characters on a black background. Hold the mental picture until you see it plainly in your "mind's eye." The ability to do this increases with practice. It is, however, always better if you can associate the figures with some appropriate object. The theory of this "visualizing" method, either with or without association, is based upon the fact (1) that many minds accept and retain a visual impression more readily than they do a mere abstract idea without a picture; and (2) that the law of association makes the mental picture (including the date) come easily into the field of consciousness, when the thought of the object suggests it.

CHAPTER XIV.

MEMORY OF PLACE.

Treating of that faculty of the mind, which when largely developed enables one to find his way almost instinctively in strange places, and which, when deficient, causes one to "get lost" in places with which he should be familiar—The subject is taken up with the idea of showing how the faculty may be developed, and the importance of training and cultivating it—Instruction, examples, and exercises are given, upon well tested and tried lines, and the careful study of this chapter should start one well on the road to a great improvement in his sense of location, his memory of places, and the ability to "keep his bearings."

Some men have the faculty of locality largely developed and are able almost intuitively to find their way in strange places. Such people never get lost, and seem to carry the location of the points of the compass in their minds without any effort. They remember places, directions, position, nature's arrangements as to space and place. Others possess this faculty in a lesser degree, and some seem to be almost without it. The last mentioned class find great difficulty in finding their way and dare not trust themselves in strange places and are constantly getting lost.

The faculty of Locality, like any other faculty, may be greatly developed by the proper exercise and practice. When the sense of Locality is but poorly developed, one takes no interest in the subject and pays no attention to it, hence the memory regarding places is deficient, the impressions recorded being but faint and imperfect.

If you possess but a poor memory for places, location, direction, etc., you must develop your faculty of Locality. To do this, you must begin by *taking an interest* in places and directions. You must pay attention and observe. Without interest you will do neither. You must look about you and notice the landmarks passed, and the direction in which you have traveled, and objects with which you have met on the way. You must look about you and *see things.* If in a city, note the corner buildings and their signs. Stand on the corners a few minutes and get your bearings. If you but put your heart in the task you will find much of interest, and the work will soon become interesting and pleasant. The trouble with you is that, heretofore, you have not been noticing things as you passed by. The man of large Locality notices these things almost instinctively, but you must start the habit by giving *conscious* attention until your mind establishes the correct habit and it becomes "second nature."

Study maps and take imaginary journeys from place to place on the map. Follow up rivers from source to mouth. Take imaginary trips on the railroad, tracing the journey with the finger. Get a school geography and get to work when you are indoors. When you are out-of-doors keep on noticing things, directions, landmarks, etc.

If you live in a large city, procure a copy of the city map and study it carefully. Start from a given point on the map and proceed to another given point, noticing the names of the streets over which you travel, and also the names of the cross streets you pass, not forgetting to keep track of the direction. Then work your way home over the same route, watching carefully that you turn the right corners, etc.

Then make the same trip (on the map) by another route, returning in the same manner. It is astonishing how this practice will brighten up your sense of locality and direction. Once in a while, memorize the names of the streets in the order in which you pass them on the map. One can get well acquainted with the city in which he is living in this way. On holidays, or other times, when you contemplate a long walk or ride, go to your map before you start and trace out the line of your trip, studying it carefully. When you then go over the same ground in person you will be continually noticing the cross streets, etc., because of your previous work on the map. A little practice of this sort will prove quite interesting, particularly if the trip is to some strange part of town.

In your study of maps, it is well to memorize them at times, wholly or in part. Look at the map and study its parts and details. Then put the map away and endeavor to reproduce it on paper, in the rough, endeavoring to note as many points of interest as possible. Then gradually add the details in their relation to each other. The object of this map drawing, of course, is to fix location and direction in your mind, and not to make an artist of you. In this practice you will find that if you lay aside the map after gazing at it a few moments and then close your eyes you will see the picture of the map in your "mind's eye." The first attempt at forming this mental picture will not prove very satisfactory, but open the eyes again and take another look at the map and fill in what you have missed in your mental picture. Then close your eyes again and fill in the missing parts. After a few trials you will be able to reproduce the picture in the mind with reasonable accuracy, when you may reproduce it on paper. Schoolboys sometimes form these mental pictures of their geography maps, and thus making their geography lessons much easier. When asked to "bound" a State, they are able to bring up the mental picture and describe it as if the map were actually before them.

This study of maps may seem to have but little connection with keeping you from getting lost or "losing your bearings." But you will find that it will so rapidly develop your interest and strengthen your faculty of location that you will be able to manifest the improvement when you are out-of-doors. Always remember, of course, to keep your eyes open and to notice where you are going, which task will now have fresh interest to you, thanks to your journeys on the map.

A story is told of an American traveler who was traveling in Europe with a party. It was soon noticed that he seemed perfectly at home in the strange cities visited, and that he not only knew the names of the principal streets, but the location of the points of interest and important buildings as well, and also the direction from one part to another. It appeared as if he had visited the place before, whereas it was his first trip abroad. When asked for an explanation by his puzzled friends, he replied that when he was on the train going to a particular city he would take out his map and guide book and carefully study them, noting carefully the general plan, the points of interest, direction, etc. He would especially note the location of the railroad station and the hotel at which he intended to stay. He would then shut his eyes and recall these points, and make the trips between them, mentally. After about fifteen minutes or half an hour he was sufficiently acquainted with "the lay of the land" to find his way about without difficulty. In this way he learned Cologne, The Prague, Old Vienna, Dresden, London City, Paris around the Opera House and other places.

After one has studied maps, with interest, they grow very *real* to him and a close connection between the actual points and the pictured ones is noticed. Remember, in practicing the exercises herein given you are developing not only the memory, but the faculty itself, upon whose ability to record clear impressions the remembrance depends.

Any faculty may be developed by interest and use. Remember this and you have the key to all self improvement.

CHAPTER XV.

MEMORY OF FACES.

Treating of the faculty of remembering the faces of those with whom we come in contact—Showing the importance of having a good memory of faces and the embarrassment attendant upon a poor memory of this kind—This chapter takes upon the matter from the cause to the remedy, and a careful study and application of the principles laid down will undoubtedly result in a great improvement along these lines—There is no attempt made to teach any "trick method," the idea followed being that an intelligent training of the faculty must result in an improvement in the faculty itself, which will in turn be the cause of an improved memory of this kind—Exercises are included.

The faculty of remembering the faces of persons with whom we meet varies greatly in degree among different individuals. Many persons have to meet a stranger several times before they recognize him at sight. And many persons seem to easily forget faces with which they have grown familiar, if the owner happens to pass from their immediate circle, for a year or two. On the other hand many persons recognize the face of any person whom they may meet, and the impression once formed seems to remain forever, subject to instant recall. Detectives have this faculty largely developed, and so have many hotel keepers, and others whose business brings them into contact with many people, and to whose interest it is to remember and recognize those with whom they meet. It is a valuable gift, as one's chance acquaintances feel most kindly disposed toward him when he readily recognizes them. And on the other hand, the failure to recognize a man may make him dislike you and may result in even gaining his active ill-will.

A deficiency in the development of this faculty indicates that the person has not used actively that portion of the mind taking cognizance of the appearance and features of those with whom he comes in contact. Such people look *at* others, but do not really *see* them. They are not interested in faces, and give but scant attention to them. The rule of "slight interest, slight attention; slight attention, poor memory," applies here. The person who wishes to develop this faculty should begin to *study* faces, taking an interest in them, and paying attention to them. In this way the power of observation is directed to features and appearance, and a great improvement may be noted in a short time. We recommend to such persons the study of some elementary work on physiognomy, which will give to the study of faces a new interest, which will result in a greatly improved memory along these lines.

To cultivate the power of observation as applied to faces and features (after determining to take an interest in them, of course,) you should study the face of every person you meet, taking note of the general shape of the head and face, eyes, nose, mouth, chin and forehead, at the same time holding the thought, *"I'll know you the next time I see you,"* which thought will cause the Will to operate in the direction of recording a clear and distinct impression.

The taking of interest in, and the bestowal of attention upon the study of the human face will repay one for his time and trouble, for he will not only be training his attention and memory, but will be obtaining an education in physiognomy as well, especially if he is using an elementary book on this last mentioned subject, as advised.

There are very few persons who can recall the features of an absent friend, and it is quite amusing to hear some people attempting to describe the appearance of someone with whom they are presumably well acquainted. Try it and be surprised at how little you really can recall, and yet you have no trouble in recognizing the friend when you meet him. Describe the eyes, nose and mouth of your best friend, if you can, from memory.

Look at the next man you meet. Note whether his forehead is high or low, narrow or broad; whether his eyebrows are light or heavy, straight or arched, and of what color; what kind of nose has he, aquiline, Roman, Grecian, pug, or what not; whether he has a large or small mouth, etc.; whether his teeth are good or bad, large or small; whether he wears a beard or mustache, large or small, shape, etc. And so on with each feature, noting the details just as if you were required to report them at your place of business, and your promotion depended upon a full and correct report. You will not forget a face studied in this way. A little practice of this kind is useful in developing the deficient faculty. And you will begin to classify features and observe them naturally, having aroused an interest in the subject. And the aroused interest means a clear impression; and the clear impression means an easy recollection.

Then practice recalling the faces of people you meet, making a mental picture of them. After you have acquired the art of recording good impressions of faces, by recalling several times the mental image of the face of any one whom you have met, you will be able to easily recognize the person after the lapse of considerable time. The repeated reviving of the mental image is almost equivalent to repeated meeting with the person in question.

You have noticed how easy it is to remember and form a mental picture of a face as it appears in a photograph or painting, and how much more difficult it is to carry in mind the face of the same person as it appears when you see him in person. It is all a matter of habit, however, and by a little practice you will be able to remember the living face just as easily as the pictured face.

We have heard the story of a '"hasty sketch" artist, who had classified noses, eyes, ears, mouths, chins, eyebrows, shape of faces, etc., and had given to each class a number. He would take a steady gaze at the face of his sitter to get the expression and air, and the general outline, and would rapidly note, mentally, the class of each feature, thus, "shape of face, 4; eyes, 8-6; eyebrows, 2; nose, 3; mouth, 4; chin, 7," etc. Your study of faces will soon teach you the several classes and varieties of each feature, and if you are studying physiognomy, as advised, you will find that the knowledge of the significance of each class of features will greatly increase the interest and pleasure in the task. We have given a number of additional examples of wonderful memory of faces and features in other chapters of this book.

Summing up, we would say that the faculty of remembering faces may be developed just as may be any other faculty of the mind, and that the secret of such development is: Cultivate an interest in faces—study them—attention will follow interest—and memory will attend upon attention.

CHAPTER XVI.

MEMORY OF NAMES.

Treating of that most important phase of Memory Culture: the cultivation of the Memory of Faces—This faculty is a most important one to every one in business and public life, and a poor memory for faces has resulted in many cases of active ill-will on the part of those whom one has failed to recognize—This faculty may be trained and developed, as well as others, and this chapter takes up the subject of this development, giving the cause of poor memories of this sort, and the best methods of improving same by training and developing the faculty itself—Examples and exercises are given, which will prove interesting as well as instructive.

The faculty of remembering names varies greatly among individuals. Many find it difficult to remember the names of even their most intimate friends, while others manifest a wonderful proficiency in the matter of remembering the names of almost everyone with whom they come in contact. This faculty has been an important factor in the success of many public men, and almost incredible incidents are related of some who have developed the same to a very great extent.

In other chapters of this book we have related a number of examples of persons possessing a wonderful memory for names. In addition to these, hundreds of well known cases could be cited. Nearly every successful politician has been forced by necessity to develop this faculty. James G. Blaine and Henry Clay owed much of their popularity to their ability to recall the names of chance acquaintances, and to call them by their names after having met them but once. Of Thomas Wharton, Macaulay says: "It was impossible to contend against this great man who called the shoemaker by his Christian name." Napoleon's wonderful memory of names and faces endeared him to his soldiers. Aristotle had a remarkably clear memory for names, and Pericles is said to have known the names of all of the citizens of Athens.

The man who readily recalls names has a powerful weapon at his command in gaining the good will of people, and it will be worth the while of anyone to develop this faculty. Memory for names may be developed just as one would develop any other faculty of the mind, or part of the body, *i. e.,* by Attention and Practice. Many persons content themselves with bewailing the fact that they have a poor memory for any special thing, and make no effort to improve it. When Man realizes that he can practically make himself over by gradual improvement, and practice, he will have opened the door to great things.

The first requisite for the development of the memory for names, is, of course, the recording of clear and distinct impressions. It is often found that it is a help to repeat aloud the name of a person to whom we have just been introduced, thereby appealing to the ear memory by a repeated impression of the sound as well as the abstract general impression of the name. The trouble with many people is that they do not *think* of the names of people they meet. They do not let the name impress itself upon the mind, the entire attention being given either to the appearance or to the general personality of the stranger, his business, motives, etc. Carelessness in this respect will invariably result in the failure to recall the name a little later on. And that is not the worst of it—by allowing ourselves to get into a careless habit regarding the names of others, we are practically losing what little name-memory we have, as nothing will so quickly resent a careless attention as the memory, which seems to act upon the principle that if its owner does not take the trouble to interest himself in a thing, it will not take the trouble to store it away with any degree of care.

If you have found it hard to revive the impressions of names, you may feel assured that it is because you have paid but little attention to people's names. Begin at once to take an *interest* in names. Analyze names; think about them; notice their peculiarities; their resemblances; their points of difference, etc. There are books published giving the origin of surnames, which are read by some people with considerable interest. We venture the assertion that no man who has ever read such a book with interest, will ever have any trouble in remembering names. He will remember them because they will *mean something* to him. He will remember them as he remembers the names of the goods he sells, or the names of anything else possessing an interest for him. Every name has its origin and meaning, and it is quite interesting to trace back a name, through all its variations to its origin. We remember a family in Pennsylvania, whose ancestors came over from Germany bearing the name of Buchley (pronounced Beekley). The grandchildren scattered and gradually adopted the spelling of their English neighbors, various changes being undergone by different branches of the family. At the present time the family reunions are composed of Beachleys, Beachlys, Beechlys, Beechleys, Beckleys, Bickleys, Bockleys, Backleys, Buckleys, Beechys, Beachys, Beachleys, Beachlys, Beechlys, Beekleys, Beckleys, Bickles, Buckles, Peachys, Peaches and Pecks. Given a few more generations and the resemblance will have been entirely lost, the dropping of a letter here, and the change of spelling there, destroying all connection. Now, we had much trouble in remembering the original name when we first heard it, but after hearing from an old member of that family a history of his family, we never had the slightest trouble in remembering the name of anyone bearing the original name or any of its variations. We also had much trouble in remembering the long German name of a merchant with whom we once had business relations, until we discovered that the name was the German equivalent for "rabbit-skin," when the trouble was over and the man's name was remembered as easily as Smtih.

We merely mention above instances in order to give you an idea of the change wrought by an acquired interest in a particular name. If you will remember something suggestive about a name, you will be very apt to have no trouble in recalling the name itself. A man named Miller may be remembered by thinking of the miller at work. Baker, Painter, Carpenter, etc., may be remembered in the same way. Names derived from those of animals may also be remembered by association, Lyon, Fox, Lamb, etc., being instances. Names derived from the names of trees are also in the rule, Mr. Cherry being associated with the fruit. Black, Brown, Green, Blue, White and Gray have an easy means of association. Bacon, Clay, Gun, Cannon, Hall, Kane, etc., are easily handled. We knew a woman who could not remember the name of a man called Hawlk, until she fixed in her mind the fondness of that man (a preacher, by the way,) for chicken, when the association of Hawk and Chicken occurred to her, and she had no trouble thereafter. A ridiculous association is sometimes the better, particularly if one has a sense of humor.

But all of the above plans are, at the best, makeshifts. The better way is to begin to *pay attention* to the names of people whom you meet, and thus train the mind to take an interest in the same, and to store away clear impressions. Force your attention upon the name, and by an act of Will impress it upon your memory. Take an interest in the name—think of it and give it your attention. Then endeavor to *fasten* it to your impression of the person's appearance. We once knew a man who would associate names with noses, his mind seeming to be open to such associations, the result being that when he saw a man's nose he would remember his name; and when he would think of a man's name he would form an involuntary mental image of his nose. After leaving the person, endeavor to recall his appearance always in connection with his name. Form the strongest possible connection between the appearance and the name, so that they will be fused. Bring up a mental picture of Dr. Street, whom you have just met, and repeat the name several times, "Street, Street, Street," fairly forcing the name in upon the image, by an effort of the will. You will find that this practice will soon result in your taking an unusual interest in persons' names, and the consequent attention will give clear impressions. The clear impressions once obtained, the remembrance or recollection easily follows.

We have found it easy to remember the names of writers by forming a mental image of the book or poem, and attaching to it the name of the writer. This plan may be assisted by always associating the name of the writer with the title of the book or poem, in speaking of the latter, thus: "Hawthorne's 'Scarlet Letter';" "Poe's 'Raven';" or "Tennyson's 'In Memorium'." This association will render it difficult to ever speak or think of the work unless the name of the writer also comes before the mind.

Many find it advisable to also get the benefit of the eye-impression, and therefore, when possible, write down the name and regard it for a moment then throwing away the memorandum. In this way they are enabled to *see* the name in their "mind's eye," as well as remembering the sound and other impressions. It is well to get the impressions of as many faculties as possible. Louis Napoleon is said to have acquired his great memory of names by this plan of writing them down. His famous uncle did not need this aid as he always connected the sound of the name with the appearance of the man. But the nephew found it impossible to duplicate this and was compelled to resort to the plan above mentioned, and by constant practice he soon acquired the reputation of having inherited his uncle's gift.

Sometimes a name, which has a tendency to escape one, may be recalled by association with a similar name, or something having some real or fancied connection. We remember once having met a Philadelphia lawyer named Townsend, whose name for some reason always escaped our memory, although we knew other people of the same name. For some reason we could never think of him as "Mr. Townsend." At last, however, we happened to think of the well known journalistic writer, George Alfred Townsend, whose *nom de plume* was "Gath." We then called our Mr. Townsend by his namesake's *nom de plume,* and after that had no trouble in remembering his name. It took only a moment to connect "Gath" with "Townsend." It has been a number of years since we have thought of this Mr. Townsend, but when we began to write the above lines his mental image stood clearly forth, but associated with "Gath" and not at first with his own name.

Plans of this kind are not the best, as a rule, and are only to be used in exceptional cases. The better plan is to *take an interest in* names. Study them—analyze them, and you will find that the increased interest will result in clearer impressions and easy recollection.

Another plan, favored by some, when they happen to "forget" a name, is to run over the alphabet from A to Z, slowly, in the mind, giving each letter a moment's attention in turn. When L is reached the missing name "Langtry" will come into the field of consciousness, brought there by the recognition of the initial letter, and the association of the balance of the name with that letter. Some vary this plan by writing down the letters in turn until the initial letter is reached and recognized. In this last mentioned variation the visual memory aids in recalling the name. The same principle operates to notify us of the incorrect spelling of a written word when we have failed to remember the correct spelling by the sense of sound or general memory.

Some have found it helpful in recalling an elusive name if they would endeavor to recall the place where they met the owner of the name, the circumstances surrounding the meeting, etc. In other words, they would try to place themselves back just where they were at the time when they met the person, and in this way they often found it easy to recall the name, which apparently came into the field of consciousness along with the mental picture.

Others have accomplished the same result by bringing before the mind a picture of any peculiarity in the person's appearance or dress.

Plans of this kind are useful in exceptional cases, or in an emergency. But the best plan is to *take an interest* in names. Study them—analyze them, and you will find that the increased interest will result in clearer impressions and easier recollection.

CHAPTER XVII.

ARTIFICIAL SYSTEMS.

Treating of the many artificial systems of memory training which have been offered the public in all ages and among all people, showing the general nature of the principal systems, and calling attention to their weak points—The history of these systems takes the reader back to the time of Simonides, 500 B. C., and shows how the old systems are dressed up and offered as new systems by their "discoverers"—This chapter will prove interesting to those who like to go back to the root of things, and then follow up the development of the subject—The reading of this chapter will enable the reader to understand the claims of many of the widely advertised systems, and will show him that there is "nothing new under the sun" so far as "patent" systems of memorizing are concerned.

For over two thousand years there have been numerous "methods" of memorizing urged by their several promoters and followers, many of which systems were for a time quite popular and which brought to their promoters much publicity and wealth. These methods, artificial in theory and strained in practice, bear a striking resemblance to each other, in spite of the fact that they originated in countries far distant from each other, and that they are separated by centuries of time. They are all based upon the laws of Association, Resemblance, Contiguity, Contrast, etc., which have been touched upon in several chapters of this book. Some of these systems are very clever, and their followers have often been able to memorize a great variety of things, the result being apparently wonderful until one is informed of the method and takes a peep behind the scenes. Anyone can commit things to memory by even a slight acquaintance with the principles underlying these systems, but the result is in the end unsatisfactory, as the systems are artificial and, notwithstanding the claims of their promoters, more or less like the "trick methods." They may aid in the memorizing of special things, but they do not strengthen or develop the memory as a whole, and in the end are apt to confuse and bewilder the mind and render weak the ordinary faculties of memory. Most of these systems have "chains," "links," "posts," etc., by which the thing to be memorized is connected with some other thing. This works for a while, and then the student finds it harder to remember the connecting links than to remember the thing itself; or he finds his attention so much taken up with the links that he forgets the original fact.

The first "artificial" system of memorizing, or mnemonics, originated with Simonides, the Grecian poet, who lived about 500 B. C. The poet was invited to a banquet at which he read a poem. Before the conclusion of the feast he was called for by a messenger, and regretfully left the hall. Scarcely had he stepped over the threshold when the roof fell in and the walls collapsed, killing the giver of the feast and all his guests. The bodies were so badly mutilated that it was utterly impossible to identify them, and the relatives and friends became most anxious about the matter, manifesting great grief. Simonides then came to the rescue, relating that he had noticed where each person had been seated, and that he distinctly remembered the same. He drew a plan of the hall, marking the position of each guest, and, as the bodies were still in the same position, they were identified by his chart. Upon this occurrence is believed to rest the responsibility for the numerous systems of memorizing generally grouped under the term "Mnemonics."

Shortly after the above mentioned occurrence, Simonides invented a system of artificial memory, which met with very great success among the Greeks. He based his system upon the idea of the seating of the guests at the banquet. His system taught the pupil to form a mental picture of a building, divided and subdivided into apartments, corridors, ante-chambers, etc. These apartments, etc., were thoroughly committed to memory, and other things which the pupil desired to memorize were associated with them. Each apartment was numbered, and in it was stored the memory of some special thing, or part of a subject. Then the next room was filled, and so on. When the pupil wished to recall the objects or subjects memorized, he would go mentally from room to room, calling to mind the contents of each in turn. An enlargement of this idea, called for the building of another house, then a whole street, etc. Some modern advocates of this system bid their pupils commit to memory the location of the furniture in their parlors, and then connect with these articles the things to be memorized, passing from the table to the chair, from chair to vases, etc. Simonides' system was afterward developed in Rome by Metrodorus, and has formed the base of innumerable systems in ancient or modern times, each promoter adding something to it, or altering it in some particular, and then announcing that he had "discovered" a new system. These "discoveries" are likely to be made for centuries to come.

Several hundred years ago Conrad Celtes promoted a system which achieved much success, and which was practically a modifican of Simonides' plan, except that letters of the alphabet were used instead of the apartments of the Greek poet's system. Toward the end of the sixteenth century Thomas Watson, an English poet, advanced a system similar to the ones above mentioned, except that he used a mental wall instead of the apartments or letters, his wall being subdivided into numerous spaces appropriately numbered. Schenkel, a German, also taught a variation of this same system, and came very near being executed as a sorcerer by reason thereof. He made a great deal of money teaching his system, until it was exposed by one of his pupils in 1619.

In 1648 Stanislus Winckelmann made a new departure in mnemonics, which has also been used as the basis of innumerable systems since that time. Although he used, in part, a modified form of Simonides' system, he went further, and originated what is now called the "figure alphabet." Each subsequent "discoverer" has used a different "figure alphabet," but for the purpose the original one is here reproduced:

WINKLEMAN'S FIGURE ALPHABET.

1	2	3	4	5	6	7	8	9	0
B	C	F	G	L	M	N	R	S	T
P	K	V	J					Z	D
W									

(Vowels, silent letters and letter "H" omitted. Two letters coming together are treated as one. Translation by sound, not by spelling.

This table was thoroughly memorized, and words then translated into figures, or figures into letters. The letters formed from the figures are turned into words by the addition of vowels, and a word or sentence constructed having some connection (real or fancied) with the date to be memorized. Some of Winkleman's successors have devised much better forms of "figure alphabets" but the principle is the same. The most absurd combinations are resorted to by the followers of these systems to memorize a date. A friend of the writer's, using the above table as a guide, remembered the date of the battle of Waterloo (1815) by the words Bonaparte Licked, the first letters of the two words being B (1) and L (5) making '15, the year of the battle. He recalled the battle of Yorktown by the words "Brave Novices Routed British," the initials "B, N, R, B" indicating 1781. To our mind it takes a greater degree of work to memorize these associating words than to remember the date itself. Winckelmann used the words BiG RaT to denote 1480, although we would have to know the event in 1480, which was to be remembered, before we could trace the connection. Other writers have worked many ingenious combinations of this "figure alphabet" idea, but for the purposes of this work, the above examples will suffice, the whole idea being more curious than useful.

In 1840 Beniowski, a Pole, taught a system in which was first introduced the "correlative" and similar theories, which have formed an important part of many widely advertised "systems" of recent years. In 1845 Miles, an American, promoted a system of his own in which, among other plans, he used sentences containing the event to be memorized, the last word of which would contain the date, according to a "figure alphabet" system. He also taught an original plan of memorizing names of important places and events by associating them with well known objects, thus: Borodino was recalled by "Borrow a dinner;" Saskatchewan, by "Sis, catch a swan," and so on. His most important departure, however, was his "nomenclature table," which took the place of the old "figure alphabet." These tables were series of words, each word of which represented a number from 1 to 100. This list when committed to memory, was applied by using a word to recall its appropriate number, thus aiding in memorizing dates, etc.

In 1848, Dr. Kothe, a German, developed a system, since largely used by other teachers, the principal features of which were the connecting of words having no relation to each other, by means of intermediate or correlative words. For instance, the words "chimney" and "leaf" would be associated as follows: "Chimney—smoke—wood—tree—Leaf." The words "Pillow" and "Ink" would be joined in this way: "Pillow—feather—quill—pen—Ink." This system has been incorporated into that of many teachers since that time. These systems, as a rule, are cumbersome, and usually prove more or less disappointing to the student seeking to develop his power of memory. Take, for instance, the well-known correlation by which is taught the word *Apfel*, the German equivalent for *Apple*, which runs thus: 'Apple—windfall—wind—storm—wrap well—Apfel." It has always seemed to us that it would be much easier to impress the word Apfel on the mind in the first place, than to remember this chain of connecting words.

About 1878 John Sambrook, of England, taught and published a system which among other things stated the principle that figures could be easily memorized by the use of words whose vowels corresponded in sound to the numerals. He called attention to the fact that the vowel sound of each figure was different from that of another with the exception of the long sound of "I," which occurs in the words "five" and "nine." his last conflict of sounds he remedied by giving the short sound of "I" to "nine," considering it as if it were pronounced *"nin."* He constructed from this principle a most ingenious system of memorizing numbers. The following words will give an idea of the words to be used in memorizing numbers from 1 to 9, it being remembered, of course, that any word of the same sound would answer as well as any of the words here used.

1	2	3	4	5	6	7	8	9
Gun.	Tooth.	Tree.	Floor.	Hive.	Stick.	Sexton.	Gate.	Pin.

In memorizing 1492 (Columbus' Discovery of America) a sentence would have to be constructed having some reference to Columbus, in which the words, Gun, Floor, Pin, Tooth, appeared in their above order, or a word would have to be found in which these vowel sounds appeared in the same order, etc., etc. Interesting, but scarcely useful as a memory developer.

The Shedd system gives as an easy method of memorizing dates, the plan of forming a word or sentence, the number of letters of which correspond to the number to be remembered. Thus to remember that Rome was burned in the year 64 one must remember the sentence "Burned Rome," the first word of which contains six letters and the second four. Napoleon's birth (1769) would be recalled by the sentence, "A strange, mighty conqueror," and his defeat at Waterloo (1815) by the sentence, "A Waterloo I found."

Other writers have promulgated systems by which events, subjects, rules, dates, etc., are readily remembered by doggerel rhymes. Some well known examples are here given:

THE MONTHS.

"Thirty days hath September,
April, June and November,"
etc., etc.

PARTS OF SPEECH.

Three little words you often see
Are Articles *a, an* and *the.*
A Noun's the name of any thing,
As *school,* or *garden, hoop* or *swing.*
Adjectives show the kind of noun,
As *great, small, pretty, white,* or *brown.*
Instead of nouns, the pronouns stand,
Her head, *his* face, *your* arm, *my* hand.
Verbs tell us something to be done,
To *read, count, laugh, sing, jump* or *run.*
How things are done, the adverbs tell,
As *slowly, quickly, ill* or *well.*
Conjunctions join the words together,
As men *and* women, wind *or* weather.
The Preposition stands before
A noun, as *in,* or *through,* the door.
An Interjection shows surprise,
As *Oh!* how pretty—*Ah!* how wise.
The whole are called *nine parts of speech,*
Which reading, writing, spelling, teach.

"SHALL" AND "WILL."

In the first person simply SHALL fortells,
In WILL a *threat* or else a *promise* dwells.
SHALL in the second and third doth *threat*,
WILL simply then *fortells* the future feat.

ENGLISH SOVEREIGNS.

First William the Norman,
Then William, his son;
Henry, Stephen and Henry,
Then Richard and John,
Next Henry the third,
Edwards, one, two and three;
And again, after Richard,
Three Henrys we see.
Two Edwards, third Richard,
If rightly I guess;
Two Henrys, sixth Edward.
Queen Mary, Queen Bess.
The Jamsie the Scotchman,
Then Charles whom they slew,
And then, after Cromwell,
Another Charles too.
Next Jamsie the second
Ascended the throne;
Then William and Mary
Together came on.
Then Anne, four Georges,
And fourth William past,
Then came Queen Victoria,
Now Edward is last.

In our chapter on the Memory of Dates we have given further examples of this kind of doggerel, which may be used occasionally as an easy means of connecting names, events, etc. Law students and medical students have a number of rhymes of this kind by which they group parts of their studies, definitions, etc.

The "figure alphabet" is sometimes used to accomplish "trick memorizing" in this way: A number of figures, one hundred or more, are written down and the slip handed to a friend. The writer then rapidly calls them off. He repeats the trick with different figures as often as desired. The explanation lies in the fact that he has memorized the "figure alphabet," and taking the words of some well known song or poem, he translates the letters into figures which are marked down. To recall the figures, he simply does mentally that which he has just done on paper, and translating the same words into figures, he of course repeats what he had previously written down. It is very simple, but quite effective as a trick.

The law of association is sometimes used to easily join together for the purpose of recollection different things having some relation to each other. Thus Dr. Watts coined the word VIBGYOR as a means of easily remembering the names and order of the primary colors, the initial letter of each color, in their proper order, forming the said word, thus, Violet, Indigo, Blue, Green, Yellow, Orange, Red. The word NEWS is composed of the initial letters of the four points of the compass, thus: North, East, West, South. The name of the vice-president who first served with Lincoln, may be remembered by thinking of Lincoln's name in this form: abraHAMLINcoln. Franklin Pierce was the fourteenth president, which fact may be remembered by his initials F (ourteenth) P (resident). We recite these things merely to show how many ways there are whereby one may remember things by attaching them to "pegs." The great trouble is that, while a few things may be remembered in this way, it is generally harder to remember the "pegs" than the things themselves, after one has burdened himself with a number of them. They are artificial, and Nature in the end revolts.

Looking back it will seem that the plan of Simonides, or the "topical system" as it is sometimes called, was the first in the field, and still shows signs of life. Then came the "figure alphabet," which is still very much with us, in a much improved form, and elaborated almost out of resemblance. The latter is quite fascinating at the start, but a little later on—well, just try it. The plan of memorizing a date by words containing a certain number of letters corresponding to figures to be memorized, looks easy, but one soon tires of it—and you are apt to get your words mixed, thereby mixing your centuries. .Very artificial! The third in order, the "associative" or "correlative" method, is interesting, but is apt to bring on mental dyspepsia if used as a steady diet by the memory. Even if these systems were practicable, they would do little more than to aid in the memory of *dates,* leaving the development of the other faculties of the mind to other methods.

The better plan is to develop the several faculties, to the end that they may readily receive impressions, and retain them, and by practice to so train the recollection that previously received impressions may readily be revived. We have tried to point out the way in this book, and we trust that everyone who has read its pages will put into practice the principles therein taught.

FINIS.